William Abdelnour

Toni!
You are a gem, lady! Thank you for reading my book. I hope you enjoy 200 pages of nonsense.
Do you think they'll be mentioning my name with the likes of Hemingway, Steinbeck, & Dr. Seuss??

Bill Abdelnour

3-13-11

The BACKYARD ZOO

PUBLISHED BY HIGH PITCHED HUM PUBLISHING
321 15th Street North
Jacksonville Beach, Florida 32250

www.highpitchedhum.net

HIGH PITCHED HUM and the mosquito are trademarks of
High Pitched Hum Publishing.

ISBN: 978-1-934666-71-5

Printed in the United States of America
2011

Dedication

For my Dear Heart (my best friend, my wife, Helen),
and our dear daughters, Jennifer and Emily,
Each of whom always told me to
GO FOR IT!

Contents

Preface

I was ten years old when my family moved from Detroit, Michigan to Jacksonville, Florida. While sitting on our back porch one afternoon, I witnessed an amazing phenomenon. Having never seen a chameleon before, I was totally enthralled with the stealth of a small lizard as it stalked a large yellow butterfly along the fence.

Using its incredible ability to camouflage itself and change colors, it proceeded to become the color of the fence. Ever so slowly, he crept towards his quarry, then, SWISH! Quick as a bullet, darted out his tongue and GULP! – The butterfly was his! With wings still thrashing – to no avail -- the chameleon chewed one strong bite after another until he swallowed the entire insect. It was lunch time at the Chameleon Café!!

Okay – So what? Well, the so what is that for most of my life I have been not only an observer of chameleon, the determination of ant, discovering that earthworm is a geophagist and has five hearts, robin, opossum, raccoon, toad, frog, snake, squirrel, spider, armadillo, cat, dog, blue jay, mosquito, and butterfly, but an interested (and perhaps, interesting) watcher of creatures, both zoological and human, both in and out of one's back yard. Here's hoping my offering – The Back Yard Zoo – fulfills that interest.

William Abdelnour

Part One

One Side of the Lecturn

Chapter 1

Sports

...Statistically speaking, the world of sports goes a little crazy...(well, okay — a LOTTA crazy!) when it comes to numbers, data, records, and stats. I mean, do we really need to know how many foul balls were hit by a left-handed batter during the fourth inning at Wrigley Field on July 10th, 1973?? Or, when the tennis match is rain-delayed 2 hours and 14 minutes, are we all enthralled with knowing about the entire blueprint and floor plan and exact dimensions of The All England Wimbledon Lawn Tennis And Croquet Club? Know what would have really been more interesting? All kidding aside — The History Channel has some very cool videos, one of which was how they make Louisville Slugger baseball bats. Truly, that was enjoyable. How much more authentic it is to hear the 'crack of the bat', instead of the 'ping of an aluminum club'.

Athletic events have always raised an interest by spectators and bettors probably since the days of the original Greek Olympic Games and Roman Gladiatorial Contests centuries ago. To our credit, we have become more civilized in promoting the ideas of 'friendly' competition, camaraderie, and good sportsmanship. [Translation: They don't (normally) kill you if you drop a touchdown pass in the end zone. (However, you will hear about it from Bill Parcells, Bobby Knight, and George Steinbrenner for the rest of the season, and for the next six months thereafter)]. I mean, if it weren't for the malcontents, how would ROLAIDS ever spell relief??

• •

History tells us that a form of basketball was played centuries ago on courts uncovered among the ruins of the Aztec, Inca, and Mayan cultures. The score was always the same, 1-0, because the first team to score was declared the winner of the contest. To the victor went the praise, glory, spoils, and borrowing from the Greeks, perhaps a laurel wreath. To the loser — DEATH — WOW! How's that for good sportsmanship, incentive, and bragging rights?! Anybody want to speak up in regard to your athletic ability?? Me neither.

• •

TRIVIA TIME:

Baseball is the only major sport in which:

- The head coach is called a manager.

- He wears the same uniform as the team players.

- The officials do not use whistles to call the game.

- Along with golf and tennis, it is postponed because of rain.

- The outfield distance measurements are different in several stadiums,... (soooo, what's a homerun?)

- And, the game is not played against the clock...

(...and, I knew you probably could not sleep tonight, unless I shared these thoughts with you...)

• •

At times, I could easily be classified the classic Sports Nut. I have my preferences and often get into trouble talking to my friends and relatives. The professionals are the culprits with their obscene salaries beyond all reason (yes, they really could support five Third World countries for two years), and setting examples like thugs and braggarts, or stupid thugs and braggarts. None of them play for fun anymore. It's all about $$$ and litigation. They make more money in six months than most people make in a lifetime because they can shoot, run, dunk, pass, catch, block, tackle, kick, skate, or hit better than most people on the planet. (So far, it doesn't sound like I'm a sports freak, does it?) But, B-U-T...The college game is the ticket. It's all about the glory and good ole' State U! The clean programs from Division 1-A down through Division III (no scholarships) are all about pride, teamwork, fun, fair play, and sportsmanship. NO, I did NOT say ALL of them. When pressure is put on them from administrators, alumni, underworld, boosters, industry, pros, and special interest groups to win at any cost — I stop being a sports nut. And that goes for the highly publicized crooks of all college sports, right on down to my own beloved alma maters.

Let's break it down: Some sports are simply not (or at least should not) be categorized with so-called friendly competition labels. Rassling (not wrestling) is not a sport. It is entertainment as phony as a $4.00 bill. Little kids do not know that difference, and their parents let them watch it week after week. Boxing — a sport?? It is brutal and a terrible 'game' to teach young people. I know, I know — 'People get hurt all da time in football, hockey, baseball, and basketball!!' Yes, they do, but that is not the object or intent of the 'game' as it is in boxing — to hit your opponent in the face, head, and body with your fists with such ferocity as often and as hard as you can until you render him unconscious...Did I get that right?? Gosh! How much fun can you have??

Tune in again next week folks when we begin our coverage of the all new Splice & Dice Spiked Wheel Rollerball Tournament! (brought to you by the Johnson & Johnson Band-Aid Corporation.) Last man standing wins a platinum gauntlet and a full suit of nickel-plated ar-mour and they really work.

• •

SPORTSMANSHIP:

In the NFL, a wide receiver catches a touchdown pass and cel-ebrates by spiking the ball and doing a victory dance in the end zone — a very carefully choreographed dance, it would seem, as he is of-ten accompanied by his team mates. The score counts, but his team is penalized 15 yards on the ensuing kickoff for excessive celebration behavior — unsportsmanlike conduct. Of course you want your team to be happy when they do something well, but that kind of behavior is not manly, or a sign of good, spirited competition. Teasing, taunt-ing, tempting, 'I dare you!', 'In your face!', smash-mouth show-off, 'hot dog', braggart, smack-talking, trash-talking, swagger-dagger — all considered unsportsmanlike conduct in the world of athletics.

Faith in my fellow man tells me that there must be more guys out there like Nolan Ryan, Bobby Jones, Michael Jordan, Arthur Ashe, and Lou Gehrig — Super athletes and gentlemen all. The story is still told of Bobby Jones playing in one of golf's major champion-ships. His shot landed in a terrible place and almost unplayable to the green. His caddy said, 'Mr. Jones, set your ball up on this nice clump of grass....no one will ever know.' Bobby glared at his caddy incredulously, and said, 'I WILL KNOW!', and played the terrible shot the best he could.

• •

Breathes there a soul so barren as one who refuses to smile, laugh, or be without a sense of humor intoto? Let's take a look at a most successful coach in The South. 'Steev' had a winning season year after year in his conference and produced countless All-Americans, and NFL stars. It would not and should not have taken very much to make him happy about all of his success. But, to see Steev in action, he would rather moan and groan about all the 'coulda, shoulda, woulda' rather than say something positive, encouraging, or humorous to his great teams. Gosh! Would his face crack if he smiled and said something uplifting instead of negative?!

Be that as it may, at least he did not spend his entire career down there, and, upon his departure, made room for others to enter the field and remember that their jobs were to teach young men values, teamwork, and sportsmanship. Oh yeah — and let's not lose sight of the fact that after all is said and done, football is a GAME! A game for which one is paid handsomely to coach, and not to berate one's own players (all of whom are somebody's son, brother, nephew, friend, cousin, husband, boyfriend), and coaches whether they performed well or poorly. Win or lose, a coach's demeanor is wide open to criticism from administrations, faculty, staff, student body, and alumni.

Whine & Cheese! Excuse-A-Rama! Sir Complain-A-Lot! Steev — Grow Up Or Sit Down!!

• •

PHILOSOPHY:

My brother, Louie — often called the Syrian Socrates — had a problem with some events being classified as sports. He wondered how a NASCAR race became a sport. A contest — yes — but a sport? Because you have a faster car than I do? That's the problem. Your CAR is faster, not you. I can beat you in a running race; therefore, let's categorize it under auto mechanics — not sport. Sadly, many spectators go to the race track in hopes of seeing a spectacular car crash. And how many people would really give a flip about the Kentucky Derby if it were not for the $2.00 bet? Therein lies the rub. First of all, your HORSE is faster, not you. Sooo, take away the $2.00 bet, and see how many people really give a damn about the Triple Crown!! Therefore, let's classify that one under gambling — not sport! Truly — I never could get too excited about a car race, or a horse race anyway.

And this from my other brother, Basil. Ya gotta wonder why the last minute and twelve seconds of a basketball game takes 13 minutes to play. Why? WHY?! (Easy, Bill — calm down — it's really quite simple. The greedy sponsors don't want to miss one single second to tell you to buy Chevrolet, Coca-Cola, Nike Shoes, Bud Lite, or Pizza Hut Pizza — that's why.) They must absolutely love overtime games. Could you cut us just a little slack there Corporate America; I mean just the tiniest tad? After all, it is already 12:40 A.M. the next morning. And ABC, CBS, NBC, ESPN, and FOX have already shown us your $2.4 million/30-second spot commercial 27 times, starting with the Super Bowl and ending not at all.

Yes, I do have a lot of my two brothers in me. They were both great swimmers, ice skaters, teachers and mentors to me, super practical, and the two best brothers on planet earth.

And speaking of great siblings, I also have the two best sisters in the galaxy. After Louie and Basil, came Gladys & Helen, and finally me — the baby. Now, being the youngest of five had its plus and minus factors. The hardest part was that I always tried to measure up to all of them — not possible.

Gladys and Helen were athletic as well. Basketball, summer camp, track team, cheerleader. More often than not, they treated me maternally. Diapers, bath, clothing, sense of humor, social graces: 'You're not really going to wear that are you?' Well, I thought I was. 'Where are you going? With whom? Who's going to be there? What time are you coming home? You have money for a phone call?' If I ever left the house without them saying 'You be careful! Have a good time!' (I always wanted to reply — C'mon, sis — one or the other!), I would have thought the world was going to end. Now that I am a 'genuine published author', they think I am the greatest thing since the invention of the wheel, ice cream, or sliced bread. You have sisters like that? Aren't they marvelous?!

I dunno — maybe there's still something to be said about sports celebrations. Just think — next time the ladies win the World Champion Horse Shoe Pitching Finals, maybe Brandi takes off her jersey again — I'm there!

• •

...Now, I'm not saying that athletic competition is a bad thing. It could be toned down a little. If, as Vince Lombardy said — 'Winning isn't everything — it's the ONLY thing!' — then, if you don't come in first, your efforts are for nought. Yes, we do need to teach our children that this is a competitive world...Isn't there room for fairness? Competing to the best of one's ability? Realizing that not everyone can possibly wind up on top?

We have to get back to basics. Somewhere along the line, people have to learn that among the many reasons to play sports, fun and physical fitness (minus the steroids, of course), ought to be near the top of the list. The NCAA makes an outstanding point on its television broadcasts: There are over 400,000 male and female athletes competing in college athletics. Overwhelmingly, most of them will go pro in fields other than sports — How refreshing.

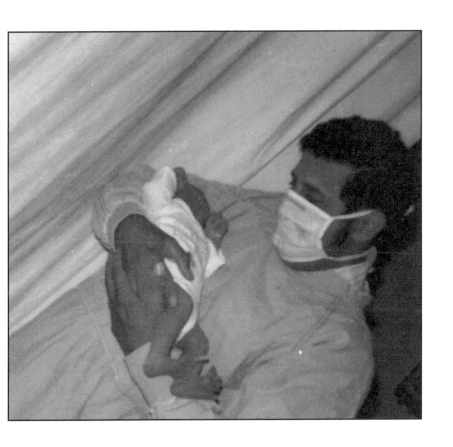

Chapter 2

Medicine

...Appendectomylly speaking, we all dread the evil malady of tox-emia entering our bods...or do we? Some of us consume edibles in portions as if there would positively be no tomorrow. Why is it we abuse our bodies so badly by diet, drink, smoke, drugs, lack of exercise; both mentally and physically; by thought, word, and deed? Why? Because we're human and stupid. Why? Because once we DO get sick, we won't admit it to anybody anyway. (Where do we sign up for Denial 101?) Why? Because (barring the hypochondriac) we all believe in invincibility – and, in alphabetical order, I am – no doubt- at the very top of that list. Here's hoping that none of us will have to look back in anger only to find ourselves turned into a pil-lar of one of those two delicious but deadly white crystals – sugar or salt.

However, in this Golden Era of high tech medical wonderment, it is indeed amazing how totally impractical our medical care systems are when we actually try to implement them. Dental Plan, HMO, Medicare, Group Health Insurance – what is the point, one wonders, when they try to make your benefit totally unreachable as if you never really ever pumped a penny into the system for the last 27 years? Bah! Humbug! And, a pox on their houses!

• •

Doctors, I'm told, take an oath upon receiving their medical de-grees, whereby they swear to uphold the ethical standards of medi-cine as given by Hippocrates, The Father of Medicine; i.e. — to make healthy the human body and to sustain it at the highest level of quality that can reasonably be expected over time...Do any of us feel justified or guilty (and only partially with tongue-in-cheek) in suggesting that probably too many of them are reciting a Hypocriti-cal Oath since too many of them do NOT have our best interest at heart, but those of dollar denominations bearing the pictures of George Washington, Abraham Lincoln, Thomas Jefferson, and Ben-jamin Franklin instead!!? Yes, money is important, but ought not be the sole factor for one entering the noble profession.

Let's start with the waiting room. (BOY! They tagged that one right, didn't they?). On those rare occasions you are seen on time, you al-most feel bad for the other patients because you know damned well that two of them were there before you. (Forget the fact that one of them has a broken leg, 106 degree temperature, and is sweating bullets). The other 98% of the time you're kept waiting 15, 20, 45, 75 minutes is because:

1. 'There was an emergency' (and hospital rounds, ya know).

2. The bridge was stuck in the up position.

3. A doctor-eating dog stood sentry at the rear entrance until animal control could arrive.'

Well now – reasonable that I am, those all sound valid to me... Sooo, naturally, when I try reversing the same lame excuses when I can't make an appointment on time:

1. 'Bad accident on highway 12 — 14-car pile-up.

2. 533 (I counted them) car train.

3. A hostile chipmunk kept me at bay for two hours'...naturally I just assumed they would sound valid to them (Gosh — I wonder why they sent me that bill for $92.00 anyway?? Let me see now...What is that? — $11.50/min. Gosh.)

"Tonight Show" host Johnny Carson once had a guest who re-layed the following: He was a businessman who got paid by the hour. He waited to see the doctor for two hours past his appointment time. Angrily, he sent the doctor a bill for two hours of his time. The unapologetic doctor says — 'You're kidding; this is a joke, right?; surely you jest'. The Small Claims court judge was no jester, ruled in the man's favor and the doctor paid him the money. RAH! One small victory for the little man! RAH...Of course, the man is probably black-listed and cannot get medical attention to this day. What price justice.

• •

Is your doctor an MD or a DO? Is he or she a GP or a Specialist? Is there a chance on this planet that you can get your teeth cleaned by an orthodontist? endodontist? periodontist? oral surgeon? Golly, I know it is a world of specialization, but within reason, please:

'Good morning, Dr. Fixum's office. Yes, he is the orthopedic surgeon. Which leg? I'm sorry, he only works on the left leg.'

'Is that above or below the knee? Oh, I'm sorry – he only works below the knee.'

'Is that a compound fracture or a greenstick fracture? I'm sorry – he only works on greenstick fractures.'

'Is that for an appointment THIS decade? Ha Ha Ha Ha Ha Ha Ha!! Oh, I see – well, you're probably trying to get hold of the other Dr. Fixxum – the one with two "X's". Ha Ha Ha Ha Ha!!

And, yes it does seem that sports medicine doctors will never run out of patients. Long live football, and all the other (so-called) non-contact sports!

• •

Don't you just love it when as soon as they come up with a great medicine, some hateful jerk does something which causes the drug company to put out a contamination alert on so and so? Tylenol, a few years ago, comes to mind. More recently, many non-aspirin products have been recalled. Celebrex (like anybody but the product's namesake could afford it anyway --- state-of-the-art for celebs --) – not safe. Ibuprofen types – non-aspirin headache, pain, fever-reliever – Aleve, Motrin, Vioxx, Advil – Safe/Unsafe? Yes/No/Maybe So? Let me tell you something, arthritic sufferers. Dr. Sugarwater's Placebo Tablets are sure things – work everytime – NO SIDE EFFECTS (or any other kind of effects for that matter) AT ALL!

• •

The most honest thing I ever heard that a doctor did was after a thorough examination and complete diagnosis of a patient, (and you know doctors – they check and probe places on your body you did not even know you had places! And, why is it that the itchy spot on your back is ALWAYS on the one square inch you cannot possibly reach – short of doing an imitation of Beauregard the hound dog backing up under the bumper of the '58 Buick sitting up on blocks in the side yard – there is no way in Hell you can scratch it!?) and still not knowing what was wrong, merely wrote GOK across his medical jacket. 'Gosh, Doc!' the anxious patient inquired. 'What's wrong? What does that mean?!'

The doctor simply said that it stands for God Only Knows!! Viva La Doctoro Honesto!

• •

...Now, I'm not saying we should all go back to cobwebs, leeches, incantations, and ginger root medicine, but perhaps those guys who first used the herbs and spices with regular success knew something we do not.

And, if laughter IS the best medicine, then maybe my dad was right: He was thoroughly convinced (with tongue-in-cheek) that a hammer, screwdriver, WD-40, pair of pliers, the YMCA and a good meal could cure the world. (Oh, yeah – and let's not forget the duct tape.)...

Chapter 3

Celebrations

...Dionysusally speaking, there is always some good time or reason to celebrate: Fiesta! Festival! Pinata! Oktoberfest! Bastille Day! Save-The-Brown-Owl Month! National Pickle Week! I mean, does anybody really need a good reason to party?! I didn't think so. The Party Animals have told us to 'Eat! Drink! & Be Merry!— Tomorrow, We...MIGHT NOT BE HERE!' (Can you even imagine?). And, if you're looking for someone to corroborate what Dionysus-The-Greek preached, look no further than to his famous Roman cousin, Bacchus. Between the two of them, they consumed more Ripple, Gallo, & Mogen David spiritus fermenti than Dean Martin, Frank Sinatra, & Phil Harris combined! (Can you even imagine?). 'You know, Alyce – we really do need to be happy & party & have a good time & celebrate the fact that little Freddy made a "C+" in conduct!' Truth be known, however, 'Kool And The Gang' said it best: 'CEL-E-BRA-TION'!!

• •

Family gatherings are always days of joyous occasions...aren't they? Well, maybe most of the time, at least. Let's take the typical (?) family reunion. OK—Sooo, the number of contacts each year increases because the family is prolific and more kids get married, newborns arrive, and lost cousins are found at a much greater rate than old timers die off; 117 in nine states at last count, and you still can't please everybody with your effort.

(1) 'My third cousin (once removed)'s stepfather's half-sister was not invited!'! 'Damn! I'm really sorry about that, but.....'

(2) 'That's only on grandmother's side – what about Aunt Hilda's life-long neighbor who runs the huckleberry farm next door to her adopted nephew, Josiah out in Scratchybush, Iowa?!' 'Gee! I really apologize for the oversight, but.....'

(3) ' I don't think it's fair that!.....'

Having been chairman of such a mammoth undertaking one time, I sympathize with ALL the putter togetherers of family reunions!

Committee and activity assignments are always interesting:

BANQUET:

'O.Beece! You take charge of the menu!' For only $19.95/plate, O. orders the following from the 'Carbo City Kitchen', one meat (pork/ beef/duck/tuna soufflé), one veggie (Brussels sprouts/cauliflour salad), seven breads, eight starches, nine desserts, and one boring mainline cola – no water, no sugarless drinks. Good choices, O!

FISHING:

Tomorrow morning's fishing expedition will be headed up by Brother Jonah – (yeah – THAT Jonah!) -- who has not caught five pounds of fish in his entire life and wants to know why hooks have barbs, and why do we need bait. (Most likely, a festive dance will be planned for them upon their bountiful return in the evening!). Interested participants gather on the beach at 5:00 A.M.

BEACH GAMES:

And, the Beach Games will be conducted by the twins, Irene and Ira Inertia – whose only claim to physical activity is that both of them have at least once caught a Frizbee (just like their dog, Spot) in mid-air, with their teeth!

So far, they have come up with the following games:

- Beer Chug-A-Lug -- Consists of five one-man teams; first empty bottle wins……..

- Aircraft Carrier Counting -- One five-man team; first team to count two ships wins...(sigh).

- Sand-Sculpture Contest -- Anything goes. No teams, no time limit, no winners, no losers, no rules – just right!

- And, last year's high-light event, Javelin Catching (winners are so rarely recognized) – remains intact...(Good Stuff, I & I!).

A feast of turkey, mountains of side dishes, non-stop football, and a gathering of kinfolk you haven't seen in a month of Sundays – THANKSGIVING! Why do people clean their house BEFORE the onslaught of dinner and relatives?? Over the river and through the woods, to grandmother's house they come. Well, let's see now— who gets the dinner idiot awards this year?

- Norman Numbskull – manages to say the most inappropriate things at all times. 'Hi, Frankie! Sorry to hear about your sister's death. When's dinner?'

- Or, Larry Loudmouth (fourth cousin – once removed) on my specialty dish — spinach dip –'Gee, Uncle Bill – I see you brought another one of your famous appetizers. What is it this time? Seaweed 'n' Caulk?!'

- Hosting 38 people for Thanksgiving Dinner is no simple task. The only bird big enough that I could find was a road-kill ostrich which dressed out at 73 pounds. Things were going very well until my smart-aleck niece noticed the tread marks on the breast. I told her to shut up and cover it with cranberry sauce!

• •

I'm not sure I should even attempt to speak of Christmas – but, I will. Are you really going to tell me that the shopping stress level is different at the mall, catalog, flea market, e-Bay, or garage sale? Nay! Say Durst! It R Alll Aw-type-ful! (I was the one you passed by 14 times thinking I was a store mannequin, when in reality, I was in a catatonic state.)

And aren't the return/exchange policies of the High-Falutin' Haven & Haberdashery, and other such swank, snobby, and snazzy stores getting tough?

1. 'Sorry Madam – you had 1 1/3 days from date of purchase to return the merchandise; your time is up.' 'But, it was a gift for my nephew in St. Louis and it's the wrong size!'

2. 'Sorry Madam – you had 1 1/3 days from.....'

3. OR – Sorry, Sir – yes I can see that your bicycle is missing the seat, handlebar, chain, and both tires. You had 32 hours from date of purchase to…….

4. OR – Sorry, Miss – your warranty expired 14 minutes ago……..Short of throwing a flambeau through the store window, how do you combat that 'you-should-have-read-the-microscopic-print-on-the-back-of-your-sales-ticket' mentality!?

5.   OR, worse, (the dreaded fly in the ointment—the coup de grace) they will only allow you to use an in-store credit slip…..RIGHT! 'Cause EVERYBODY can always use another $47.00 12-foot wicker basket hand-made in Botswana!!

• •

…Now, I'm not saying that we celebrate and party at the drop of a hat, but have you noticed how many hats, caps, helmets, bonnets, fedoras, and berets have hit the deck in recent times with a really good time to follow? You're right – it doesn't take much for most folks to cut loose, let down their hair, and have a good time. Does that mean sing, dance, eat, and drink to an excess? To the point of being obnoxious-fall-down-drunk? Of course it does! Really? Well, it does make one wonder if the old adage of 'all things in moderation' just might not apply in 'this' case. (You pick the case.)

Chapter 4

College

....Graduatorally speaking, a sheepskin will always be a prized trophy and possession for one who completes a course of study in any of the academic disciplines. Why not? The rigors of pursuing a diploma or degree in college are strenuous and demanding to say the least.

At any given time, we all wondered why some assignments and policies were made, or deemed necessary at all. 'But, I'm a history major – why do I need chemistry?' Did it matter? NO. Why? Because Professor La-di-da said so. We moaned and groaned, but, by golly – we did those assignments and turned them in on time. Quality? Wellll, don't press it...(Magna Cum Laude – what else?) This diploma says I did it and I WILL hang it on the wall!

• •

Never considered a scholar, I entered every academic institution and program on – you guessed it – probation! Oh, how I wish I had paid more attention in high school. Having no idea of how to take notes or study, I must truly thank my buddies for getting me through college algebra and chemistry. Otherwise, I never would have made it through by myself. And, needless to say, my efforts were less than totally successful; therefore, I was in and out of school three different times (albeit for lack of funds more often than not), and finally earned my B.A. degree 7 ½ years later.

Some of my professors were rather interesting. It was annoying to me that some of my early professors thought they were so cool, not because of their ability, but because of their association with so-and-so.

For example: One math professor (Mr. Troopyon), insisted that everything he taught the class was 'So simple! The formula is so basic! Why can't you understand it!?' Mr. T. was so impressed with the fact that he had Harvard University after his name, AND was co-author of our required curriculum textbook. My, My – how wonderful to be not ONLY Ivy League, but 'Crimson' as well.

Likewise, a professor of humanities (Mr. Peedersun, who certainly looked the part with his typical scholarly appearance: Ivy League haircut, horn-rimmed glasses, narrow rep tie, tweed coat and leather elbow patches – well, la-di-damn-da!) took great de-light in slamming American institutions   such as college football and jazz music:

1. 'Football!? You call that sport? Organized war is what that is!'

2. 'And to your jazz music, which employs that typically lewd American instrument – the saxophone- I say disgusting!'

Sooo, to the greats on sax – John Coltrane, Charley 'Bird' Parker, Gerry Mulligan, Boots Randolph, Paul Desmond, Bobo Edwards, Stan Getz, Grover Washington, Richard Elliott, Boney James, Kenny G. – and countless others, please allow me to apologize for Herr Peedersun. Similar to our 'Harvard Grad', Peedersun was an 'Oxford Grad', quite British, and to be perfectly honest, a genuine snob!

And, thirdly, an English professor (Mr. Allosyn) – took great de-light in slashing and pulverizing freshmen themes and essays, as if every 18-yr. old were destined to be the next Steinbeck or Hem-ingway. It seems his only claim to fame was that his nephew once pitched for the Cincinnati Reds. Yes – we heard about it more than once. Not surprisingly, none of us ever remembered asking them; all three gentlemen gave such advice and comments freely and un-solicited. Duly impressed, insulted, and gracefully, we managed to stifle a yawn or two. Whatever happened to qualification, modesty, toleration, and compassion in the classroom?

On the other hand, there were (are) some super teachers in col-lege, too. You know the ones – a vocabulary so mammoth, it would not only choke a horse, but send all Webster employees deep into a thesaurus! We were thoroughly convinced that our collective pro-fessors of Asian, European, African, American, and Latin American history were – if not first cousin kin – at least personal friends of Buddha & Confucius, Charlemagne, Napoleon, & Churchill, Shaka Khan & Haille Selassie, Ben Franklin & Teddy Roosevelt, Mont-ezuma & Simon Bolivar. Such vast knowledge & analytic skills were absolutely mind-boggling to those of us fortunate enough to have such outstanding college teachers. Yes, it was often a case of 'If you did drop your pencil, you might as well drop the course!' At times, my buddies thought I lived in the library. I truly cannot recall EVER going to bed on the same day I woke up. Midnight oil was burned on a daily basis, often re-fueled by peanut butter, Ritz crackers, and/or gobs and gobs of cold pizza.

Right off hand, I cannot think of anything for which I would have traded those trying, turbulent, truly terrific days of college life. I grew up a great deal during those 7 ½ years of school.

• •

ROOMMATES:

Envy – that deadly sin – often took over my brain when I witnessed the ease with which some of my colleagues made their grades. Two come to mind: My dear friend (Jag) graduated with a 3.3 GPA. So what? Well, he was a psychology major and did all of his research and wrote all of his papers without ever stepping foot in the school library!! THAT'S WHAT! Further, he had time to pledge a fraternity, play poker on a weekly basis, and dated the prettiest girls on campus in the process. Drove me crazy. Another roomie (Dan) – math major – could, on a regular basis, play bridge, puff on a stogie, and work calculus problems SIMULTANEOUSLY – and still earn a 3.7 GPA. Drove me crazy. Were it not for my buddies Jag & Rudley, with their great sense of humor and encouragement, I would have gone crazy. We still have mini-reunions together every year. An absolute delight!

• •

REAL GRASS:

Do you remember the second semester of your freshman year? Yes – the one when you took 18 credit-hours? And, Thursday's schedule started at 7:40 A.M., ended at 4:30 P.M., and lunch consisted of a package of crackers and a Pepsi-Cola on your way to 4th. hour, and included a 3-hour lab in chemistry, and 4:30 P.M. was when the campus sprinkler system came on, and you had to play 'Dodge The Water Canon' to get across campus??? Well, so do I!! I often wondered if a lawn sprinkler really required the strength and range of an atomic-powered bazooka! Were they trying to water the grass, or kill any and all forms of alien invaders!? Got soaked on more than one occasion. Felt good on September 10th. – froze my buns off on January 10th.! Why were they still on in January?? I think 'because' is the best we can do on that one.

•••••••••••••••••••••••••••••••••••

ATHLETICS:

Just why did you ever take a date to a college sports event? If she didn't keep you hopping for popcorn, hot dogs, soda pop, pretzels, peanuts, and nachos, she was asking: Why would anyone want to steal a base? What's a first down? Is an inning the opposite of an outing? Why is that a free throw – does he have to pay for the rest of them?... Whoops – Sorry ladies. I'm sure you've had some geek go with you to a swimming meet only to hear him say rudely and unsolicited(ly) – "Oooh...breast stroke and freestyle – those DO sound interesting!!" OR "You mean those ladies play beach volley ball in bikinis?? Allll Riiight!"...Okay, you win. I apologize. Please forgive me.

•••••••••••••••••••••••••••••••••••

HOMECOMING:

How happy could the alumni be when good ole State U. scheduled a game with the college equivalent of the 12-time Super Bowl Champs and watch their team get clobbered 72-6?? What were they thinking? Next year – a friendly game of shuffleboard, or, perhaps – Fusbol. And don't even start with me about the excesses of college sports: Funding, title this-that-n-the-other, amateur/professional – Fact is that some athletes CAN read, write, and count. Therefore – baseball, Chevrolet, apple pie, motherhood, and College Sports! I'm still there. GO TEAM!

•••••••••••••••••••••••••••••••••••

GOING TO COLLEGE:

Ever help a friend or relative pack up to go to college for the school year? Well, I tried to help my daughters, Jenny and Emily, to do just that. We started in April for a move in August. (Check me on this, but didn't the Spanish-American War take less time than that??) Well, anyway, their idea of packing was to attach a trailer hitch to the house and pulling it all the way to Tallahassee!! They were there five days and we'd already sent them another box of more necessities, and they wanted a second box sent which included a request for some colored Manila folders. I said, 'Ladies – you are 200 yards from the University Book Store, across the street from Bill's Book Store, and just down the road from Target, K-Mart & Wal-Mart' (both since re-named the Jen-Mily Mart). They said, 'Yes, Dad – but they're all out of chartreuse, vermilion, mauve, fuchsia, and puce!!' Did you know there is a color named puce?? I didn't know that. Nor did I realize, heretofore, that our entire economy is wrapped up in paper, cloth, glass, plastic, sneakers, Kleenex tissue, and panty-hose!

• •

THE GUYS:

Nothing I say about the Back Yard Zoo would be complete without a few words about the best friends a guy could ever ask for – The Guys. For lack of better terms, we'll call them The Springfield Boys and The Southside Bunch – all brought together between ages 10 - 15 via Sunday School, Scouts, Summer Camp, High School and College Rivalries.

On any given Friday night, three, four, or five of us would be without dates. On those rare occasions we DID have dates, our famous beach parties were our signature activity and standard fare: chicken on the grill, play guitars, sing songs, run out of beer and purple passion, go home...still wondering why those girls never went out with us again!

Chollie and I had some very famous fishing trips together, mostly in the surf:

1. One time we went – 12,000 square miles of beach. Chollie took one cast; two steps into the surf, he stepped on a fish hook right in his big toe! I laughed – Chollie cussed.

2. Another time we went – same 12,000 square miles of beach – I took one cast; two steps into the surf and got stung by a jellyfish! Chollie laughed – I cussed.

In high school and college, Chollie's house was always home base for everybody, all the time. His mom and dad thought about adding a wing onto the house just for us...My mom tried to adopt Chollie just so she could see me more often. When we were at Chollie's house (9 days/wk.), their grocery bill must have been $200/...A DAY! Gosh, his mom had patience.

Sunday basketball game at Southside Bunch High School...outside, hard concrete court, cold, windy. Jorj says, 'I think the locker room window is unlocked...let's sneak in and play inside the gym.' Sooo, we did – Jorj, Lobbert, Chollie, Rilf, Timmy, Cobble, Vic, and like a genuine dummy, I went along with them. Nice inside! Hardwood floor, no wind, sun shining through the windows, having a good time!...The lady across the street saw us sneak in. Ten minutes later, two squad cars, four cops, and the Dean of Boys, Mick Hayser walked through the gym door. We froze, and, of course, all blamed Jorj: 'Good move, Jorj!' Lucky for us, Mick Hayser knew everyone of us, either from the Southside School he was recently assigned, or from the Springfield School from which he was transferred. He saved all of us from going to Juvy Hall, or Raiford. Chewed our fannies out, and said GO HOME! Mick Hayser always took care of his boys.

Mid-'60's – Some of us were married – some were not. The gang had gone into various directions and professions – law, engineering, dentistry...but Chollie and Abbey, we cooled 'em...we knew where the big bucks were...we went into teaching!! And, I'm sure Chollie would STILL recommend a career in education...if you like poverty.

On our famous camping and fishing trip to the Keys, we learned two things: Yes, fish and pelicans ARE smarter than people; and yes, the mosquitoes down there DO have a pilot's license! Chollie and Jorj hitched their jungle hammocks to a billboard sign (no trees on the coral rock Keys). Cobble and I tried to sleep it off in the car. Between the heat, and fighting the insect aircraft, we lost, laughed, and left. We STILL did not catch any fish. Who but Chollie, Jorj, Cobble, and Abbey could strike out in the Florida Keys, Marineland, and Sea World?? We never caught more than five pounds of fish altogether between all of us! REALLY bad!

Another camping trip. Same guys. Breakfast: 18 eggs on the griddle – one breaks. Cobble: 'Hey, Chollie, your egg broke! Jorj – your tangerine's rotten! Lobbert, Abbey – your biscuits burned!' Never happened to Cobble's food – always someone else's.

Early years of teaching, Chollie and I were both single and anxious to see the country. Sooo, we camped out for a month on a trip around the USA. Grand Canyon, Yellowstone, Dodger Stadium – (saw Drysdale and Koufax) – Disneyland, Candlestick Park…saw the great Willie Mays get a base hit, steal second base, and make a patented sensational catch in centerfield…all by the third inning, only to see Mays get sick and have to leave the game in the third inning. I looked at Chollie, and he said – 'Yeah! Right! Whose luck is that?!'

Next Stop: Who but Chollie would say 'Abbey — Let's go to Europe!' I said 'Great! Let's Go!' We were the only two bachelors left, both had a few bucks in our pockets, and both of us were history buffs; (and, being teachers, we both had the whole summer off). We went. Stonehenge, Roman Forum, Colosseum, Eiffel Tower, Sistine Chapel, Berlin Wall, Parthenon. We went to a bull fight in Madrid. Too cheap to buy seats in the 'sombre' (shade), we sweltered in the sun. We cheered for the bull. Learned FAST you don't do that in Spain. Sooo, we learned quickly to say 'Si Amigo! Bravo! Ole'! Vive El Matador!...Somehow, it just didn't seem like a fair fight to us.

A few of us still keep in touch. But, mostly we have fewer opportunities to be with "The Guys". Wedding bells, military, college, moving to new towns, job opportunities, simply growing older and less able and death itself. Would I love to see that old gang of mine collectively one more time? Is grass green? Does Sunday follow Saturday? Would "The Guys" literally give you the shirt off their back? Do you still have a group of friends you'll remember fondly the rest of your life? I'm thoroughly convinced you know exactly what I'm talking about. Friendship – There is nothing quite like it on the face of planet earth. Take good care, my friends, and savor the moments.

• •

...Now, I'm not saying that a Cap 'n' Gown gives you license to be smug, obnoxious, and treat your fellow man with that 'Better-Than-Thou' attitude. However, you do recall that feeling of superiority you had on Graduation Day. In reality, most of the 22-year old grads on that day realized basically one thing: They didn't know very much about anything at all. It was only the beginning of their work-a-day world. That's why they call it Commencement, Johnny!...

Chapter 5

Military

...Logistically speaking, we all try to do the right thing, in the right way, in the right place, at the right time. But, that requires logic – a branch of the psychological disciplines not always employed by the military. I mean, after all—why do something the easy way when you can find any number of ways to confound and complicate it?

It hardly seems to matter if the orders from headquarters come from the military academies (Army, Naval, Air force, Coast Guard), or from the 90-day wonder boys of OCS, ROTC, Warrant Officer System, or The Pentagon itself – confusion reigns. From The Joint Chiefs of Staff, to the commanding officers of each military branch, to the non-coms, to the grunts – (Gosh, it DOES sound like the old gossip game –TELEPHONE – whereby the original message of 'Synchronize your watches' ends up sounding like 'The tent is made of swatches'!) Could be that filtering on down through 17 layers of Chain-of-Command that simple communications comes out somewhat distorted. But, then again, could be that, just maybe, it's because the Pentagon is a five-sided structure... you know, convolution and all that...(By the way, ever tell a marine that the USMC was little more than the police force for the USN?? Be forewarned – DON'T!)

● ●

One of the few cases in which the Cold War Soviet Union was allowed to use a bit of humor in poking fun at its own soviet system was in the field of journalism, not exactly famous for its view of freedom of the press. The two largest circulating newspapers in Russia at the time were the state sponsored and state controlled "Pravda" and "Izvestia". During the midst of that dour period, one brave Russian writer dared and managed to get a good laugh while addressing a group of scholars and bureaucrats with this comment: 'Well, as usual – I see that there is no Pravda in Izvestia, AND no Izvestia in Pravda' – (there is no truth in the news – no news in the truth.)

I love the USA and served proudly in Uncle Sam's Yacht Club for a few years. I was a 21-year old kid and had just successfully completed three straight semesters of college with a 1.8 GPA. I was quite convinced that I was not intended for academia – at least not at that juncture in my life. Sooo, I joined the navy. I believe in military service to protect America's right to enjoy a "Pravda – Izvestia" joke without fear of retribution.

The rank and file in the military is an absolute howl at times. Do they really have to treat EVERYBODY like they have the IQ of a paper clip?? Or, they, themselves, of half a paper clip?? Basic training in Ye Olde Boot Camp AND aboard ship made most of us feel like puppets. My buddy, Shillts from Kansas, stood with me at second day muster and we were quite hopeful that our CPO, Doogle, was about to pronounce my name correctly: 'AB'! – I said, Shillts – so far so good. 'DEL'! – Shillts said, Abbey – I think he's going to make it!…'BANORF'!….We looked at each other incredulously, thinking – how could anyone blow a four-letter syllable like NOUR and come out with BANORF!!?? I should have known – Hell had NOT frozen over yet.

My brothers, both 15-16 years older than I am, served in World War II, and both were independent grocers after the war. Always concerned for their little brother Billy Boy, they often sent me "care" packages. Without exaggeration, one afternoon, Shillts and I were sitting well out of view from the rest of our company unit and managed to polish off the better part of : a pound of Zenobia pistachio nuts, a large jar of pickled pigs feet, a package of Oreo cookies, four cans of Vienna sausage, and four candy bars. It was a wonder we did not get sick and it was truly one of the most fun-filled days we both had in our entire enlistment.

Another swabi friend – Frellish from Montana – on the never ending task of painting EVERYTHING aboard ship one shade or another of haze gray paint. Chip paint, scrape paint, sand paint, prime paint, paint paint, re-paint: 'I got it, Abbey – this is all in preparation for us for when we do go into combat, we'll pull up alongside the enemy and then we'll — PAINT them to death!!'

Yes, I know – you did not think guys from Kansas and Montana (and my good buddy, Herry from Nevada) even knew we had a coastline. Me too. But, they were really good eggs and I miss them and hope life's been good to them.

CHOW:

It is just tradition among the armed forces that personnel complain about the food in the military. But friends – let me tell you – 'it just ain't so'. My years in the Navy were marked by great chow – aboard ship and/or any shore facility. At one time or another we had dishes which included salmon, rabbit, duck, venison, veal, wild boar, and lamb. While anywhere near the California coast, we gorged ourselves on apricots, olives, pineapple, avocadoes, and plums. Euphemistically speaking, some of the navy dishes had some rather unfriendly labels (which I shall spare the gentle readers) given by the 'Old Salts' — chipped beef on toast, minced beef on toast, tremendous variety of cold cuts, and delicious stuffed bell peppers and rolled cabbage. Cussing all the way through the chow line and all the while being ribbed about putting side boards on their trays — while they loaded up each meal just in case of the famine...if anyone went hungry in the Navy, it was his own fault.

• •

DISCIPLINE:

I suppose that in order to whip 65 individuals from all walks of life, into one cohesive military unit, you really must have the attitude of — Do what I say, When I say, How I tell you, Don't ask questions OR Talk back – EVER! Sooo, because I had a few years of college, could read, write, and count, I was made Company Yeoman (secretary) — in charge of roster and roll call, schedules of classes and activities, watch assignments, etc. My one and only benefit? I carried a clipboard and bayonet instead of a heavy rifle all through boot camp.

None of us ever fully understood why reveille was at 0430, to shave, get dressed, muster on the grinder, and stand in line for breakfast TWO HOURS LATER!! 0430 was bad enough, but let's be sure to compound it with the following: Approximately 0200 hours we are all awakened for an 'emergency' fire drill. 'Emergency' — translation — we don't know who pulled the false fire alarm, so EVERYBODY roll out and line up. 'When we come bah, hold out yo hands.

The 'culprit' will be caught 'cause the alarm sprayed a solution on his hands and it will show up under the ultra-violet (or is it infra-red?... anyway, almost Nancy Gear) light!'

Well, now – guess who just happened to polish his shoes the night before, (and shoe polish does not wash off or out from under one's fingernails readily in the shower)? Yup! ME! It looks just like the alarm substance which was supposed to be the tell-tale sign of the guilty 'culprit' and, of course, I was addressed by the CPO: 'Well, Ab-del-banorf — sure looks like you're the one who pulled this little stunt and we gotcha!' I said 'Sir! That's shoe polish!' Sooo, after his entourage finally convinced him that it was indeed shoe polish, Doogle – without a word of apology – dismissed the whole company and said go back to bed! CPO Doogle was more often than not a bleary-eyed drunk, unkempt and stupid — paper clip I.Q., which just might be an insult to the paper clip!

• •

Human perspectives during World War II were quite different than they were during the Korean, Vietnam, or Iraqi conflicts. Not only was national support for the war effort almost unanimous, but the news media coverage was mostly objective, informative, and entertaining. Is there anyone who lived during the 1940's who did not look forward to the reports and cartoons of Ernie Pyle, Bill Mauldin (Willie and Joe – Up Front), and Sad Sack? Walter Winchell? Drew Pearson? Edward R. Murrow? We get an almost feeling for that era by the likes of Dik Brown's "Beetle Bailey" comic strip today. Go Get'Em G.I. Joe! Hubba-Hubba! Kilroy Was Here!!

How big a treat it must have been for all the sailors, airmen, soldiers, marines, and coasties when the great USO shows came to entertain them. Hope & Crosby, Martha Raye, Jerry Colonna, The Andrew Sisters. Year after year – World War II, Korea, Vietnam, almost until the day they died. Talk about a morale booster – especially when they always came with a bevy of beauties to give the troops a little eye-candy now and then.

...Now, I'm not saying that we don't need a chain-of-command. Perhaps, however, it would be better and better served if all the links were pulling in the same direction!! There is a legendary (if not documented) account of an incident which supposedly happened in the 1930's just before WW II began. It seems Mussolini's Italian Air Force was attacking the totally overmatched African country of Ethiopia. One strafing plane swooped down on a village, and in total desperation, a tribesman threw his spear at the plane, and miraculously, the spear stuck in and jammed the plane's engine — flame out — crash... True or not true, plans do not have to be complicated beyond all reason. (Yeah – I know: 'Line up for spear issuance and spear-throwing instruction!'). We get enough SNAFU and TARFU by accident without actually planning things that way. Lessons in futility ought not be part of the military curriculum. 'You understand me, boy?! Turn to! Square that hat, sailor! Hurry up and wait, soldier.!'

Chapter 6

Music

...Euterpestically speaking, lyric and melodic poetry should be pleasant to the ear. The muses were interesting creatures. They could be whimsical or stern; understanding or punishing; reasonable or completely unreasonable. How much faith does one put in the gods and/or the muses of life?

The abilities of both man and nature to produce an infinite number of sounds is astonishing, and the old adage of 'judge not lest ye be judged' does not always apply.

Euterpe could make one wonder if he/she played favorites, or merely played favorites.....

Here's to the 88 sounds of eleven octaves. Pianoforte!

• •

I love music. Rarely does my car ever get as far as the end of the driveway without my CD player/radio/cassette player being turned on. But, place your bets ladies and gentlemen. Are all endeavors of Euterpe (the muse) pleasant to the human ear? YE GADS! Oh, to be a dog at times and selectively hear only a few extremely high notes produced within some of man's creative combos.

In another time and place, perhaps less complicated times of history, music was written, played, sung, heard, appreciated. It made people ponder, smile, dance, happy, angry, sad, feel uplifted — spiritually nourished, laugh, cry, think because it was intended to do those things. Today, some of that is still true. However, some forms of the clef and chromatic simply make one wonder — just what on earth were they thinking?! Is anyone really going to try to tell me that today's art form known as 'rap' is little more than a variation of jumping rope in the 1940's-'50's to 'Mabel, Mabel, set the table – don't forget the RED HOT PEPPER!', at which time the end players would twirl the rope at such a fast speed (not quite Double Dutch) that the jumper would trip, fall, scrape two knees, and break one femur??!

Where's the talent?? Where's the skill? Anybody who can count to four in 4/4 time, and SAY (not sing) something that rhymes can do a rap:

'LIFE is MISERABLE and FILLED with PAIN --

LOOK outSIDE, it's GOING to RAIN;

TELL me DARLING how's your LEG?.....

I BROUGHT YOU AN EASTER EGG!! Ra-ra-ra-ra-ra-ra-ra, Ra-ra ra-ra-ra-ra-ra.

Slap it on some seedy CD - go platinum.

• •

It should be with a tremendous sense of pride that one stands to hear or sing his National Anthem played or sung...Have you heard some of the renditions of The Star Spangled Banner during the '90's? Of course you have. Rozann Barrr? For real?! Mickey and the Mono-tones? What? Are you kidding me? If that didn't make you cringe and your skin crawl as though it were the scraping of fingernails, or chalk on a slate chalkboard, or a fork on a cast iron frying pan, then I miss my guess, and maybe all the words are supposed to be broken up into eleven syllables each, and sound nowhere near the original melody and lyrics. Gosh-- in this high tech world of electronics, could we not all benefit from a few doses of Stevie Wonder's synthesizer?

Today, I'm partial to jazz, classical, broadway, and the Oldies I grew up with in the '50's and '60's. Every generation's music is simply the greatest. For me it was Elvis, Brubeck, and the Maestros of classical music. I still have my modest collection of 45's, LP's, cassettes, and CD's over the decades. If it is all ever converted to CD's like all good do-bees hope, it will be an absolute miracle. My good friend, Al Birt, was a collector of 45 RPM records; 75-100,000 of them at last count before he died. My nephew saw his collection one time and responded with only one word – AWESOME!! Truly it was. Some of the good stuff has lingered and endured as greatness. I mean, does it really get any better than Glenn Miller, Benny Goodman, and the Dorsey Brothers, Tommy and Jimmy? I don't think so. Still, other pleasant surprises have cropped up in new forms which tell us that YES – there are still tons of un-tapped talents out there on planet earth. Who knows? Maybe I'm one of them.

I always wanted to play the piano. Not LEARN how to play, mind you – just sit down and play.   Not   learn, not take lessons, not practice, not drill up and down the scales – just play... Stupid, right? Right! Always admired people who could play and tried it twice semi-legitimately. It is so much more difficult than one might think. Still, maybe someday. In orchestral music, I've always been partial to the cello, tympani, and the French horn. How mellow their sounds are to my ear. How expertly they were applied by Mozart, Handel, Bach, and Beethoven. The classical, romantic, and baroque stylings of music are often imitated but incomparable to this day. From the overly fussy, highly ornate works of Handel ("Water Music Suite", "The Messiah"), to the humorous comment made by the Prussian King Frederick reacting to a piece of music composed by Mozart that there were 'Too many notes! Too many notes!'

How delicious the sounds of the creators of music and all those who emulate (or try to emulate) the patterns of the past. Here's to music – the food of love.

                    Do. SOLFEGGIO!!
              Ti
           La
        Sol
     Fa
  Mi
 Re
Do

...Now, I'm not saying we all make beautiful music. But, you know – making music is really quite simple sometimes. We have all invented our own motto, slogan, single-jingle, ditty, verse, or poem. We feel and claim ownership. ' I, my, mine, us, our, -- this belongs to ME!' So, just how do we go about proving that? We give it a label, tune, or a melody...wail it out on a kazoo, or comb and tissue paper. We hum, sing, whistle, grunt, -- tap it out on a table or a spoon. We got rhythm !! Author, composer, musician.

Early on, if man could not send a visual message by smoke signal, he did it by sound.   Early man made melodic sounds drumming on an animal skin, or hollow log, blowing through a ram's horn, river reed, or conch shell. It's no wonder that music became a form of communication, and to this day is STILL considered an (the) international language.

Chapter 7

Choirs

...Musicologically speaking, if you don't sing or dance in the shower, hum along to the car radio, harmonize at a campfire, beat out the rhythm to your favorite CD or cassette, (45's, 78's, 8-tracks, or LP's {33 1/3}, or you've ever been lucky enough to see, have, or hear a gigantic Broadcast Album – approximately 18" in diameter, and rotated at a whopping 16 RPM – long enough to play a complete opera, concert, or symphony, for those of us who are truly antiques), or try to hit a church note which is far too high or too low for you, then, you are probably a statue! Does music have the charm to soothe the savage (or human) beast? I don't know. The next time you encounter a raging grizzly bear – hum a few bars of "Claire de Lune" and see...I suspect we'll hear from you if it works. In the meantime, think back on any one of your favorite choir directors and see if he or she is not somewhere in the following descriptions, situations, or temperaments.

• •

(Garvey Tyler was organist and choir director at the Presbyterian church for 10 years. When the Methodist church offered him a very attractive and hard-to-refuse position, we did not have the heart to lay a guilt trip on him (...but we did anyway). Garvey Tyler is truly one of God's good people. We love & miss him.)

Let's pick on our choir director, who is leaving us to move on to greener pastures (insert your own definition of 'greener'). We've all been through a few choir directors. But, before we start, Garvey wants me to make a few announcements...He was just pondering: Did you ever stop to think of the fact that 8 out of 10 is 80%? OR, that Garvey Tyler spelled backwards is relyT yevraG? OR, that if you spoonerize his name it is pronounced Tarvey Gyler? OR, that this weekend, that's THIS Saturday and Sunday, will be followed by Monday, Tuesday, and Wednesday???...If not, then he wants to know just what in Hell you do in your spare time??!!...For Goodness Sake!

Garvey got a little careless the other day and left a copy of his new Methodist church job contract on top of the piano, and I couldn't help but notice some of the highlights. Check this out:

First of all, he has an entire suite of offices on the 82nd. floor already named The Tyler Tower, and of course, a breath-taking view of the beautiful St. John's River. WOW! Can't beat that with a stick!

Furniture? Mahogany desk, – credenza – solid oak; grand piano; leather chair with arms; computer; and telephone with ALLL of the 800 toll-free numbers to three planets!!

He gets a brand new Lamborghini; receives a $225,000 bonus just for SIGNING the contract; his music budget is something like $7700 /week; AND a special clause which guarantees him 3-hours/ day Jacuzzi time!!

In contrast, when he came to the Presbyterian church, I think he was given a pencil, a yellow pad, a cardboard box, and three torn copies of "Jesus Loves Me!" AND the tenors and basses had to share a copy because Rob and Rolan (former baritones, wouldn't ya know) did not know the words!!

I mentioned this to Pastor Tym, and he said 'Yeah, Bill, I know and we're workin' on it'...[Translation: The new choirmaster will get TWO yellow pads!]...Not much of a mystery why Garvey's leaving.

• •

Gosh, Garvey – what a motley crew you inherited for the last ten years. Look what you got:

- Pastor and Mrs. Pastor...Of course, thank God for Steffie; she's the only one who can really keep tabs on Tym. At supper, I noticed she gave him a swift kick under the table and said: 'Tym! Please slow down...I don't want Angelo to put up a sign outside of his restaurant that says: Angelo's – favorite spot of the Faster Master Pasta Pastor!!

- And then there's Rob "The Clerk", always reminding us that he signs the checks......Anyone in the choir ever get a check from Brother Rob?...I didn't think so. Of course, Caty "Moneybags" lies to him about the money; he never knows how much money is in the treasury anyway! So, let's thank God again, this time for Janie...She's the only one who can keep tabs on Rob. However, she's running out of things that work and may resort to violence...

- Then, of course, there's Patti...ranking member of the city's-Poll Cats. Patti wants to be sure we spell that P O L L, otherwise that hand she always has on the pulse of the city may start to tighten.

- We have TWO Wolves...ever try to teach a wolf to sing? Vickie says Rolan practices all the time at home...and it's hard to tell if he is a wolf, coyote, or fox!

- Katie...the most powerful distributor of food in town, so you folks lining up at the food pantry incognito – Fuggedaboudit! You can't fool Katie-type!

- And of course, Sweet Shirl, our very own Queen of Computer Keyboard! Remember back when Herbi wanted to change the name of the church because it sounded 'tooooo military'?? Well, Shirl goes one better...She wants to re-name the church "Our Lady of Cyberspace and All Angels Dot Com...!!!"

- Add King Richard to the mix, and the truth is, Rich and I are the only two in the choir who don't know G Sharp, from Gee Whiz, G-String, or Jesus!! Poor Patti gets stuck between us – we hit a sour note, she gives us DOUBLE elbows! Rich? Three cracked ribs. Me? In traction for 7 – no, 9 days! I'm still trying to catch my breath!

- Our Soprano Par Excellence, Dotinell...You may not remember, but at Emily's wedding, we wanted Garvey to play, Dotinell to sing. Well, wouldn't you know it, they argued for 45 minutes whether it should be A Capella, or accompanied by organ; A Capella! Organ! A Capella! Organ! My Dear Heart, Helen, grabbed me by the arm, and said, 'Bill, please, get up there and sing 'Blest Be The Tie That Binds!'

- The Original Swiss Miss, Klaudya...nothing like making it an international choir, AND Terpsichorean Delight!! Klaudya's other half, Jay, is the epitome of steadfastness. Actually, it you looked in the dictionary at the word STEADFAST, you'd find a picture of Jay. They often wondered, I believe, if any of us had any vocal chords. Their anger sometimes became quite vocal: "I get more music from three acorns and a twig!!"

- And, finally, there's that one Uppity Episcopalian, Bill...who can afford to be irreverent as Hell, because he's not even a member of the church!!

• •

Now, let's talk about Garvey...Everyone thinks he always, AL-WAYS has such a mild, pleasant demeanor. Well, let me tell you, friends, there have been times when he was NOT so pleasant. We should have suspected something the first time he walked into the church, wearing full beard, a monocled eyebrow, and carrying a riding crop. His first sentence was: 'Achtung! I haf vays of making you seeng!' 'Sunday morning 9:15 does not mean 9:16 and 2/3!' Sometimes he became a dictatorial chameleon, by changing accents on us...'We don't neeed yo kahnd 'round here'! Every red-neck within three miles of the church applauded.

Just the other day, I called the National Park Service just to find out if there was any truth to the rumor that on the flip side of Mt. Rushmore they are going to carve four more faces...this time of 20th. century tyrants; yep, you guessed it – Hitler, Castro, Hussein, and TYLER!! They said, ' What rumor? It's in stone!'...

He really does have quite a repertoire: He's equally comfortable playing Ellington, Shearing, Basie, Brubeck, Scott Joplin, OR Haydn, Mozart, Bach, Beethoven, OR Elvis, The Beatles, OR Ricky Martin... Well, talk about a Wannabee, – might as well go for broke, right?

Ever notice how he starts off each piece of music? Most guys would simply say "let's take it from the top"... Not Garvey; his term? 'Let's run it'! Run it!! Sounds like a man with lots of experience at traffic lights.

Remember a few months ago, how we all felt so sorry for Garvey when he had his little fender bender? Hurt his hand? Ohh, Poor Garvey–! How was he going to conduct the choir? How was he going to play the piano & organ?? Well, I won't say that Garvey has a lead foot, but the last traffic ticket he got read: 'Speeder finally stops! Found with foot and accelerator in carburetor!...Can't wait to see him in his new Lamborghini!!'

How about his gentle way of dismissing your "constructive criticism", as he says.... Get lost, Choir Dog! If I want static, I'll buy a cheap radio! When I want your opinion, I'll give it to you!!

And, I love the way he starts us out on a brand new piece of music...he hands out a musical work of 17 pages, and what's the first thing he says?: ALL RIGHT, everybody turn to page eight!... Now, you have to wonder – what on earth did the first seven pages do to offend him?? Gosh, Garvey! – lighten up! They're only sheets of paper!

Believe it or not, folks, I got to choir practice EARLY one night, and heard Garvey rehearsing his famous vocalizing warm-up drills... You know the one that sounds so innocent?; "Where Shall I Go-o Today?" Well, seems the original lyrics go something like this:

> I killed five sopranos today-ay,
>
> The altos are not far away-ay,
>
> You tenors & basses can't stay-ay,
>
> I killed five sopranos today (one more)
>
> I KILLED THE WHOLE CHOIR TODAY!!!!!

My, My....Such bloated egos Garvey had to endure: Saucy, Sarcastic Sopranos, Altos with Attitude, Testy Tenors, and Brazen Baritones and Basses. And, because we are that choir, I have written An Ode To Garvey:

> We've patted a pan, and kumbled-a-kee,
>> And, Garvey, how strange those sounds were to me!
>
> Quarter-note, half-note, fermata and staff —
>> This limited choir sometimes made you laugh!
>
> Soprano and alto, and tenor and bass —
>> With baritone sounds often giving the chase.

We may have been up-scale, we may have been down —
And, yet, you did smile – you NEVER did frown!

You nodded and sighed, at times quite concessional,
And wondered, I'm sure, at that ragged processional.

So, now to the Methodist, from Church Presbyterian,
Don't forget us, the gang, and one Super-Syrian!!

God bless you, my friend. We hope they know what a gem they are getting! We love you.
Vaya Con Dios, Garvey.
You're one Helluva Guy!!
We'll Miss You Whole Bunch & Lots!

(The following is a short list of English musical terms translated into Garveynese…It just might help (if you don't know Garvey very well)…)

ENGLISH DICTIONARY OF MUSICAL TERMS | GARVEYNESE LEXICON de MUSIQUE:

Bill Abdelour, Editor

TERM	ENGLISH	GARVEYNESE
A Capella	Without Instrumental Accompaniment	Oh, stop your belly-achin' ANYbody can sing The Messiah, Bach's Christmas Oratorio, and Beethoven's Ninth Symphony without benefit of keyboard!
Allegro	In a brisk or lively manner	What a starfish does when you break off one of its legs...
Bass	The lowest, deepest voices & sounds in music	Base, vile, ignoble drones

TERM	ENGLISH	GARVEYNESE
Bb	Half-step note between A natural & B natural	Well, O.K., but for the ladies - not a good idea! (?)
Canon	2-3 voices covering each in rotation; an exact tracing of music &/or lyrics	Huge gun weapon used to blow away tone-deaf choir!
Canticle	Liturgical song (e.g., The Magnificat) taken from The Bible	What a feather on the bottom of one's foot can do...
Carry-over	Do not breathe for three measures...	Do not breathe until next Tuesday!
Copyright	Protection of one's original written material (literature, music, etc.); must have author/publisher permission to reprodue	I have the right to copy anything, anytime, any amount, any reason I want! Trademark/Shmademark! You leave me alone! I'm a nice person. Buzz Off!
C#	Half-step note between C natural & D natural	Yeah, but the same goes for touch, hear, taste & smell!
Contrapuntal	Polyphonic; counterpoint	Contrary to all expectations, we're going to kick on third down...(?)
Crescendo	A swelling of volume in sound of music	I WANT THE RAFTERS TO VIBRATE!!
Do (see scale)	First note of 8-note octave or scale	I'm worth MUCH more of this than you pay me!
Fermata	Hold note until choir director gives cut-off signal	Hold note until you turn blue, or better yet, - PURPLE!
Fugue	A contrapuntal musical form or melodic chase	Careful not to mispronounce this one, friend... you'll be in a lot of trouble!

TERM	ENGLISH	GARVEYNESE
Half-rest	A moderate pause in the music	The other half? - PRACTICE!
Half-step	Go up or down one-half note	Try not to trip on your choir robe
Kumble Kee	Vocalizing the scale with initial sound of "K"	A bumble bee (and major stock-holder in Kaiser, Kraft, and Kellogg Korporations).
Let's try that again	Let's try that again	You sound exactly like HOME-MADE HELL!!
One more	One more vocal progression up or down on the scale	I Lied! — So, Sue Me!
Page turn	Difficult point in music to be quickly picked up on next page	The point at which a low-life gets his chance to eat after the knight and squire...
Prelude	Organ/piano music played prior to church service	This is my time to show off - so just stifle it!
R	Letter & sound coming between Q and S	Does not exist in the world of choral music
Run it	Let's take it from the top	Let's take it from the top, but I will stop you at every other measure
Scale (see Do)	Eight successive notes beginning with 'Do' on the 8-note octave	You STILL don't pay me enough on scale, base, minimum wage, salary or commission or otherwise!
Sucker spot	Point in music where one can be easily fooled into wrong note and/or timing	Store where one can buy Blow-pop, Tootsie-pop, Sugar Daddy, or Holloway All-Day...

TERM	ENGLISH	GARVEYNESE
Tapes	Recordings paid for by choir members to hear various portions of Christmas Program but still not delivered...	Just Hush! I spent your money on 7 CD's & a new bottle of piano polish — SO WHAT?! Besides, my credit's good! Whatsa matter?...You accusin' me of somethin' dishonest? Don't you trust me?? All left-over moneys will go toward the Garvey Tyler Retirement Fund ANYway...SO THERE!
Tenor	Sound range between baritone & alto	Tenor, eleven or twelve — you're STILL not on key!
Treble	Musical clef written for soprano & alto	We got treble, friends! I say treble right here in River City! Now that starts with T and that rhymes with P and that stands for POOL!
Zumble Zee	??????????????????	Now DON'T get cute with me!!

• •

...Now, I'm not saying that choir folks & choir directors are peculiar people, but damned if they don't behave in some of the oddest ways imaginable. They say (always that indefinable they)... that some of the funniest things in life happen in church. No argument from me. I can't be the only one who has actually been teary-eyed over some hilarious situation from the choir, congregation, or pulpit. Ofttimes (do people still use that word?)-, Ofttimes, the music had to be delayed until we all stopped laughing so hard and regained our composure. Truth be known, my talents are limited. Although, I can carry a tune, play the harmonica, and the radio – my tunes are usually carried in a bucket, and I thank my patient compadres for their indulgence. Organ! Piano! FORTISSIMO!

Chapter 8

Telephones

...Telecommunicationally speaking, perhaps (just perhaps) AT&T and the entire Bell System should have been one monopoly that we left alone, and perhaps (just perhaps) we would still be enjoying the quality of affordable services we enjoyed in the 1950's and '60's. The telephone bill had only two entries: (1) regular local telephone calls, and (2) long distance telephone calls.

Today, one needs two CPA's and three attorneys to decipher the charges he receives from any of 87 different carriers in any given month: 'Hello. We're here to serve (or is that slam?) you. For any questions concerning your monthly statement, please contact our customer service office.'...Well, now. That sounds simple enough. Shouldn't take more'n a couple of Acts of Congress to get to talk to a real live person. I know I can hardly wait for that opportunity. Standardize and simplify, my friends. Nothing has to be that complicated.

In the final analysis, the very funny Lily Tomlin as Ernestine the telephone operator (1960's TV show – Laugh-In) was hilarious and right on target in making us aware of the futility of trying to talk to a large corporation.

• •

TELEMARKETING:

Raise your hand if you hate telemarketing as much as I do...ALL RIGHT!! I, too, have signed and registered my name to be taken OFF those confounded lists several times, only for some clown to find some clever way to get around the rule because 'it is for a noble or altruistic cause, or in the public's interest.' Since when does a vinyl siding peddler qualify as a noble cause?? Why do I have to hear a pitch from the Fraternal Order of Police which is NOT sanctioned by the FOP?? Seems to me that enough responsible TV news coverage is broadcast to let me know that a quarter-million victims of a disastrous tsunami qualifies as a worthwhile project without some telemarketer telling me that I need to contribute to a bogus account which, no doubt, will simply line the coffers and pockets of his crooked and greedy scheme. And NOW, I'm told, there might soon be a way for the telemarketer to call YOUR cell phone, AND charge YOU for the unsolicited call! Gosh, I can hardly wait for that one…Just who is paying these people $6.50/hr. to sit at a telephone all day and be a nuisance? And, yes, I have tried the reversal — 'Yes, I see, — well, OK then, how about you give me your phone number so I can call you back tomorrow night at 6:30 PM, and interrupt YOUR dinner. Better yet, give me your address and I'll come to your home so I can waste a full hour and forty minutes of your time. In other words, get a life, get a job, get the Hell off the telephone, and stop bothering people!'

Am I the only one who equates such harassment to the door-to-door salesmen who hawk their religion (you know — the ones who think and act like they invented the faith) and pamphlets as if they were fabric cleaners and tooth brushes?? 'But wait — that's not all — for $19.95, you also get three free catechisms, one easy-release pass from purgatory, AND the all-new revolutionary automatic, three-in-one, left-handed Frit-Benzer!' Martin Luther, where are you??!

Quite literally, I nearly put my fist in one young man's face because, after I asked him nicely to be on his way, he insisted that I make a commitment to the Lord and refused to leave my front porch. I am not famous for my patience. Hackled and bristled, I prepared to engage in fisticuffs with the over-zealous one, when finally, his more aware partner convinced him to leave the premises and pedal (peddle) on down the street! Could these be the same self-righteous jerks who would not allow their families to watch Super Bowls "X", "XX", or "XXX" because they were rated "X"?? NO DOUBT!

…But, I digress — How fond are we of and thankful for that marvelous invention — that touch-tone automated telephone service?: For English, press 1, for Spanish, press 2, for Dravidian, press 3 & 2/7, for Interplanetary Galactic Antennae Arc 'N' Spark, press 9316Q (direct line to those who tend to migraine, ulcer, apoplexy, and busted blood vessels). Let me get this straight, now — someone convinced them that this was better, and more efficient (or at least less expensive) than letting me talk to a real live person. Is that it?? What was I thinking?! And it only took me an hour and 12 minutes to find out that my check had cleared the bank 11 days ago. G.E. said it best: Progress Is Our Most Important Product. Tom Edison lives!!

CELL PHONES:

The new cell phone owner is always a most visible (and audible) delight. Normally, you can encounter them at the grocery store or Super Wal-Mart — pick one. It's either Larry Loudernhell, or Donna-Mega-Decibel who's calling home: 'HEY SUGAR PLUM — DID YOU SAY TWO EGGS & THREE BREAD, OR TWO BREAD & THREE EGGS?? THEY ONLY SELL EGGS BY THE DOZEN, YA KNOW!' Or, 'WHAT BRAND OF ANTI-PERSPIRANT/DEODORANT (condom, tampon – same-same) DID YOU SAY TO GET?' Now everybody in the store knows two things about you: you have a cell phone, and that you took an overdose of Dumber'N'Hell pills this morning. IDIOT! Has to be the same poor soul who REALLY thinks driving and talking on the cell phone is okay. Just for the record, it isn't. Stats have shown time and time again that doing so is one of the major causes of car crashes.

I still search for a company that will sell me a cell phone that will allow me to call a party, and receive a call from a party, without all the fluff — I don't really need one that is a computer, takes digital photographs in 3-D, stores and plays all the music of The Big Top 40 since 1950 and 64 of your favorite CD's, gives the baby a bath, prepares dinner, and can fire ICBM's and interplanetary galactic missiles just in case of WW VIII!! Just make a call, and receive messages...Is that so hard? There just has to be another definition for progress.

And, dammitall anyway — you can hardly find a pay phone on the streets anymore because E_V_E_R_Y_B_O_D_Y has a cell phone! Too bad they're not equipping the new cell phones with a few brain cells as well.

• •

Ah, yes – modern technology. So advanced that all of Ma Bell can be shut down by merely turning on a dial-up computer (about which ye dare not ask me since my sum total knowledge of computers rests in the fact that I can spell APPLE!) Long live electronics and silicon chips! And you thought a virus could be held in check by antibiotics! Shame on thee and the powers that be! TSK! TSK!

• •

...Now, I'm not saying we can or should divest ourselves of this revolutionary invention. But, is that what Alexander Graham Bell had in mind when he was merely trying to find a way we could talk to each other without being face to face? I find that hard to believe. Today, the large corporations and government know more about us than we will ever know about them. Ought not be petrified every time the telephone rings, bracing yourself for some ominous and threatening rank and file slug telling you that your service will be cancelled, AND, you will surrender your first born child unless your past due balance of 44 cents is paid in the next eight minutes...I mean, 1984 has come and gone, and GOSH! It's STILL true! BIG BROTHER IS WATCHING YOU!

Chapter 9

Commercials

...Propagandistically speaking, a modicum of truth would be nice if sponsors really expect people to watch and listen to their commercials. Cynics, like myself, thrive on tearing those advertisements apart. If, indeed, an advertisement is designed to create a desire to purchase, why do we derive so much pleasure from merely poking fun at them and finding fallacy after fallacy in our observations of them? Now, I understand, that since so many viewers are blocking, or video advancing, or muting through so many commercials, the big boys are paying movies and television programming some big bucks to show, use, and/or refer to their real products by brand name in a script, because Archie is not likely to go to the restroom, or make a sandwich, just because an actor is opening up a bottle of Coors beer right in the middle of the plot. Even before the main feature begins, product commercials occupy much of your viewing time. There is a move underway to produce television commercials which will prevent Carl/Cathy Consumer from muting, advancing, or blocking their messages... Good ole American ingenuity.

I remember a professor I once had in a course in economics opened his first day by saying something like: 'Nothing ever happens until somebody sells something.' I guess it's true; product, service, idea, sex, reminder, candidate—shrewd, clever, subtle publicity, but propaganda, nonetheless. And, another popular idea – if you have it, a truck brought it...Are we still looking for Jimmy Hoffa?...

• •

Just an interesting tidbit: In that same economics course I just mentioned, the following was offered: – Each year, approximately 10,000 new items are brought out on the market (many of them battery operated); of that 10,000—2,000 will actually be looked at by industry; of that 2,000 – 800 will be considered for production; of that 800 – 200 will be patented; of that 200, only 60 will actually sell; and of that 60, only 12 will witness a profit...No wonder the competition is so fierce.

Some folks have told me that I missed my calling; that I should have gone into advertising instead of teaching. I find it positively amazing that at any given minute you turn on your television set, you are more likely to see a commercial, instruction, promotional, programming schedule, or public service announcement before you see any actual programming! And, don't even start with me on election year campaigning! Fortunately, my Dear Heart (Helen) has, so far, prevented me from throwing a brick through the TV screen each time I heard…'and I approve this message'.

• •

Ever walk into a gas station to buy one gallon of gasoline for your lawnmower? It's advertised price (circa) $3.99 AND NINE/TENTHS!!! Who are they kidding? How absolutely insulting to one's intelligence that you can buy the gallon for less than $4.00…Who came up with that one? And, why??

• •

Love the way everything is always presented as being 'new and improved'. Makes one wonder – how bad was the stuff I was using last month, or yesterday? Often, what is 'new and improved' is the packaging. The formula for aspirin has not changed in a hundred years. That miracle drug is so multi-purposed and versatile, that if it were invented today, it most likely would require a prescription rather than being available over the counter.

• •

Many moons ago, Ivory Soap advertised that it was 99 & 44/100% pure…Pure what?

They never told us. Since they also advertised that 'It Floats', it makes one wonder if perhaps it was PURE AIR! Which is terrific if one was in the market for oxygen! (And, whatever happened to the other 56/100%? Let' see now – broken down to its lowest terms, that would be…28/50…or no, that reduces down to 14/25 of one per cent…Who knew???)

• •

Some ads are so 'subtle' that you don't even know what they're selling until the end of the commercial. Jeans? Popcorn? SUV? Jell-o? Perfume? So many of them are selling an image and don't really care if you like the commercial or not, as long as you remember it. It seems to me that since Madison Avenue is buying 16-18 minutes of a 60-minute program, they ought to care a little more if they offend Carl/Cathy Consumer or not; including an insult to their intelligence.

• •

Sooo,— just what is it that qualifies a bottle of olive oil to be labeled 'virginal'? I'm told that olive trees — like apricot trees — have both male and female species. Sooo,- 'he' gets fresh, and 'she' responds: 'Stop that! I'm not that kind of tree!' Then, there's the brand which boasts that it is EXTRA VIRGIN OLIVE OIL — No, please — don't tell me — let me guess: 'I'm not that kind of tree, but I will mess around a little!!'

• •

Do Viagra, Levitra, Cialis, et al REALLY have to caution us about a possible 4-hour erection?? Are you kidding me? If you have a 4-hour erection, my friend, then chances are that sexual performance is not your biggest problem. Common sense, please. I cannot possibly be the only one who is extremely tired of bedroom and bathroom products incessantly hammered into the living room, family room, or den non-stop, 24-7. And for goodness sake — please get someone who speaks English to sell your product, service, cause, or candidate.

TESTIMONIALS:

- Is it really a good idea to have the NRA tell us what a great new water pistol/rifle has been developed by Joe's Aqua Weapons that's coming out just in time for Christmas?

- Let's hear it for the Double-Edged Samurai-Old Timer-Case-Barlow-Buck-Bowie-Swiss Army Knife/Sword as seen on TV and endorsed by O.J. Sympsun'!!

- We don't want to forget the encouraging words of Olliver Obese and Frieda Fat-Lots: 'Say, Kids — make sure Mom and Dad take you to Bardee's tonight to try out the new artery-clogging, 2 & 3/5 pound Enormous Burger. You can either eat it, or inject it directly into your heart!!'

- Normally, the celebrities who plug all of these television products most likely know as much about it as (or less than) John Q. Citizen; and, poor things — after all, they're only making $34 trillion/ minute — hate for them to miss their next meal.

- One of the most offensive weapons on television commercials is their use of disclaimers: 'People who have no lungs should not use Benz-O-Matic SCUBA gear.'

- What's next? — Viktoriy's Seekret advertising a training bra for your 11-year old?

(Not recommended for girls measuring less than 22-inch bust).

• •

My favorites are the ones which prescribe some pervasive and/or invasive medical product or procedure and then tell you in a very authoritative and comforting voice that: Some possible side effects might include baldness, change of race, growth of second navel or third nipple, male pregnancy, or loss of thumbs!! ALWAYS, the recommended — 'If you have questions about da-da-ra check with your doctor first...Right — How easy that is. 555-1234. R-R-Ring. Hello, Dr. Fixxum?...

• •

The producers of these great, expensive, convincing, and nauseating commercials are well-versed in using just the right jargon and catch phrases on their prey. Check out the usage of: fresh... (anybody ever advertise stale doughnuts?), free, bargain, half off, weight loss, smooth skin, lovely hair, revolutionary, youthful, economic, roomier, pre-owned...(wonder how many used car buyers bought into that one?), hurry — limited time offer! while they last! two-for-one! one to a customer! easy, strong, labor-saving, just in time for (pick a season or holiday), first come — first served, safe, popular, and so the scare tactics continue ad nauseam and ad infinitum.

And, about that 'easy' claim — ever see a house painter on television taping off, or cutting in the wall from the ceiling? around fixtures and cabinets? just above the baseboard? dangling from a ladder twelve feet in the air?!? NO! always on the easiest, smoothest, eye-level, largest, flattest, wide open, no obstacle, wall surface so accessible that anyone's pet goldfish could accomplish it! Likewise, the 'easy-to-use' vacuum cleaner — NEVER under the roll-top desk or sofa, drum table in the hard-to-reach corner or behind the large TV console; OR the lawn mower— NEVER along the fence, house, shrubs, bushes, or around the flower beds and trees, but the wide open space of the largest part of the lawn that anyone could train a billy-goat to do!...Hell — the billy goat just might do a better job than the mower anyway!

• •

The Marlboro Man always encouraged every man to think for himself.....Must be why the Ad Biz uses all of the following euphemistic gimmicks: so you can think for yourself:

- Avant Garde/Cutting Edge – If there's a complicated, unworkable way to do it, we'll find it.

- Chic – No one over 22-years old would dare wear or be caught dead in this outfit.

- Deluxe – Very Expen$ive.

- Economy Size – It takes three people to lift it.

- Industrial Strength – will remove any surface, i.e., porcupine quills, cactus needles, paint, thorns, tree bark, brick, asphalt, or sidewalk (as well as skin, lips, and eyebrows).

- In Vogue – Let's make sure we all look, think, speak, and act exactly alike, as if we were all made on a doughnut machine.

- Money-Back Guarantee – Yeah! Right! All lawsuits on the spindle, please.++

- Only A Few Left – Either they only had four to begin with,

OR, they're still trying to dump 12,826 of those blasted two-handed, mechanical widgets.

- Portable – Any item (smaller than an 18-wheeler) with a handle on it.

- Subtle – If you've figured out the name of the product we are advertising before we get to the punch-line, we have not done a very good job...(Same technique municipal government uses in euphemistically calling the city's garbage and trash men sanitation engineers).

- ++ Time-Honored — We have managed to win every lawsuit brought against us for the last 13 years, including the ones on the spindle. (Thank you, Nancy Stahl!)

- Unique – Only 358 other companies manufacture this same item.

- Water Clean-Up – Requires steel wool, sandpaper, acid solvent, elbow grease, and fourteen hours of labor.

The envelope, please: — And The First Annual Television Commercial Insult-Your-Intelligence 'Crumby' Award goes to...

• •

...Now, I'm not saying that television commercials are a total evil. They are not. Especially since they help pay for free programming to John Q. Some of them are actually honest and well done. I still find it fascinating that no beer commercial ever shows anyone actually drinking the beer. Only the tremendous appeal it has for lovely ladies, hard bodies (six-pack abs, of course), and panache. C'mon folks — Diogenes is STILL carrying his lamp, and STILL searching for an honest man.

Down through the decades, truth in advertising has taken a beating. Let's resurrect it and give the viewer and listener a chance to make an informed decision about la-de-da. And now, a word from our sponsor. (Ohh, how about 'castle'...that's a pretty good word...)

Chapter 10

Awards

...Recognitionally speaking, awards, rewards, and presentations have long been part of the world in saying, doing, and giving nice things to people for a job well done. That is a perfectly acceptable fact and practice. We all need and enjoy strokes. It is the excessiveness of awards which make it a travesty of good taste. When one takes a good idea and grinds it into the ground, it's no wonder people react and over-react.

They don't all take place during the sweeps and ratings month of February. But, there are certain times of the year when the airwaves are totally saturated with awards shows, many of which are totally inane, and which John Q. does not even recognize or care about watching. Each of those industries spends too much time glad handing, back patting, applauding, oohing & ahhing their own fellow workers. A bit of temperance and a little more effort in selection of quality would be so welcome a change.

• •

I truly cannot count how many different awards shows there are on television:

' Live! From Mozambique! The Academy Of Scaling Trees To Catch Flying Rodents (just as a dog catches a Frisbee in mid-air) presents the Seventh Annual 'Squirrely' Awards Show!'...To recognize excellence in various fields of endeavor is a good thing. To do so for the mundane, absurd, obscene, and to strictly profit from such P.T. Barnum tactics is pure, unadulterated hokum. Why on earth do we need award shows for every single category of music, drama, fashion, broadway, musical, movie, video, radio, advertisement, commercial, public service announcement, news, TV show, volunteer, cable, public works, classical, beauty, journalistic, jazz, Little Theater, sports (sure – Sports Illustrated's swimsuit issue qualifies as sport...), sales, song, transportation, poetry, modeling, literature, Caldecott, Newberry, Pulitzer, Nobel, and My-Dog's-Better-Than-Your-Dog contest on the planet?! Yeah...Right...Well, there I go again – asking as if I don't already know the answer is $$$! And, do we really need Miss America, Miss Black America, Miss Teenage America, and Miss Nude America? Miss USA, Miss World, and Miss Universe? Grammy, Latino, and Country Music Awards? R&B

Video, Hip Hop Video, and Rap Video Awards? People's Choice, Golden Globe, Screen Actors Guild, Oscars, and Emmies? Gosh, if they continue to spend all that time patting themselves on the back, each one gushing more than the other ('Monique, m'love! You are sooo deserving! I'm soo glad you beat me and won!'...[Translation – 'I'd like to scratch your eyes out!!')], how will Madison Avenue ever collect on all those intelligence-insulting commercials they manufacture? Yeah...Right...Well, there I go again...

(I hear the smart money says that this year's winner for Album of the Year will definitely be The Bloodfest Quintet starring Snake, Slice, Slash, Spike, and Sizzle.)...And as the anticipation builds...

• •

Other sources have said it much better than I, and justifiably so, have come up with their own awards:

One William Proxmire, Senator from Wisconsin from time to time would present the Congressional Golden Fleece Awards to too many shysters who ripped off Uncle Sam with controversial &/or questionable purchases of ungodly prices all paid for by the U.S. taxpayer – From toilet seats, to hammers, to furniture, pillows, and wash basins. He made Americans aware, drop their jaws, and laugh like Hell at our own fiscal foolishness.

In the 1960's & 70's, "Laugh-In's" Dan Rowan and Dick Martin called our attention to folly by their weekly presentations of the 'Fickle Finger Of Fate' Award. Embarrassed does not begin to describe the uncomfortable feelings the most deserving recipients felt during their broadsides, and Voltaire would have been delighted.

Mindful of David Horowitz's consumer show in the '70's – whereby he always told his audience to 'Fight Back!' – John Stossel (ABC's 20-20) does yeoman's work on exposing, in his own words, 'Hucksters, Cheats, & Scam Artists' – all the while alienating the 'Liberal Media'. His signature and book title say it all (although the book is not entirely palatable) – Give Me A Break.

• •

And aren't the acceptance speeches getting special? Some of them can hardly wait to use the lectern as a format to expound a deep-rooted political or religious belief which does not concern most viewers and/or listeners:

- 'I truly believe that the current acreage designated for the new mental hospital should be re-located in order to save the rare gay and lesbian ant colony now found on that property.'

- Then, of course, if one does not have a command of the English language (and I don't mean foreign recipients) then he or she resorts to the most vulgar language you can imagine. !*X@"XX!

- Let's make sure I thank alllll the appropriate little people who helped me earn this award: Mail Room Marvin, Dominick-The-Deli-Delivery-Guy, my ninth husband, Schuyler, the SCAR (Society Currently At Risk (?)), my pet ferret, tsetse fly, Venus Fly Trap, and the TAIJ (The Academy of Idiots and Jerks), all of whom contribute tremendously to the AGNF (Arthritic Grasshopper Nest Foundation).

• •

With these examples, I know I am not alone in thinking that maybe having access to 847+ channels is not a good idea. Quality air time is too quickly giving way to boredom, repetition, and very bad taste in choices – if, indeed, that is what they are. Maybe we should offer REwards for those bounty hunters of such pabulum award shows which rank (and tank) right up there with those so-called 'reality shows'. HELP! STOP THE BLEEDING!!

...Now, I'm not saying we should not recognize excellence, or outstanding performance in these various fields. I've just always taken pride in being a practical man which prevents me from being able to justify the occupation of three hours and twenty minutes of network time, and holding one's breath to see who finally gets the Best-Zydeco-Squeeze-Box-Quintet-Made-Up-Entirely-Of-Left-Handed-Three-Fingered-Red-Headed-Cajuns-Who-Make-The-Hottest-Red-Beans-And-Rice-This-Side-Of-The-Mississippi-River-Award!!! (The envelope is right there under your napkin.) Jambalaya and Crawfish Pie!!

Part Two

Another Side of the Lecturn

Chapter 11

National Honor Society

...Lexicographically speaking, the English language is one of the most difficult on planet earth. Who better than the super-qualified scholars of The National Honor Society to demonstrate a mastery of the language in a fashion which does nobleman's work and serves 'Brother Webster' ever so proudly? They think. They speak. They do. If only they, themselves, could understand what their penchant is for knowledge, then maybe collecting Dollars for Scholars would not appear little more than a handout for college-bound spoiled little rich kids who can read, write, speak, and count.

They are annoying at times, but, more often than not, they are a sheer delight to teach and discuss their bright-eyed and bushy-tailed aspirations in life. These are some of the fun things I've had the pleasure of doing (and teasing) with NHS during 32 of my 33 years at Fletcher High School.

• •

(MOST OF THE FOLLOWING SEGMENTS TOOK PLACE AT THE ANNUAL NHS INDUCTIONS):

My! My! Such an impressive group of platform guests:

All of these fine NHS officers;

Ms. Jardeau – Teacher Of The Year;

Ms. Monn – Fletcher's Principal;

Dr. Shure – NHS Sponsor...All Bona Fide members of NHS...

...And then there's me...And, here I am...Second-generation Syrian and the eternally grateful Honorary member for 32 years, and Co-Sponsor of the Fletcher Chapter of NHS...Honorary — that's because my report cards were always a stellar evaluation of 'C', 'C-', 'C+'... the only reason I knew the letters 'A' & 'B' is because my last name begins with those two letters, and my mother threatened me within an inch of my life if I didn't learn to spell it by the time I was 18 years old!

Just before the induction ceremony tonight, I was talking to a couple of inductees in regard to their hopes, dreams, plans, and concerns for the future. I THOUGHT they were going to say something about trying to make a 4.0 GPA, hoping to get into Stanford, Duke, or MIT, or, perhaps discovering a cure for AIDS or cancer; maybe becoming CEO of Microsoft... But, uh...NO! One Senior Girl said — 'Well, tomorrow is Groundhog Day , and I was just wondering if Punxsutawney Phil would see his shadow !!'— Gosh! Talk about major issues of the day! One Junior Boy said — 'Well, I'm still wondering where the light goes when I close the refrigerator door!'— Soooo, you can see we have some REALLY sharp, deep-thinking kids coming into this chapter tonight.

• •

NHS INDUCTION:

Once again it is my annual pleasure to take part in the NHS Induction Ceremony...and, I never cease to be amazed at the enormous amount of gray matter these folks have in high school.

Their versatility is truly remarkable, and range from all things Animal, Vegetable, or Mineral...to all things Solid, Liquid, or Gas...The Arts & Sciences, Technology, or Humanities.They even do well in the abstract...Poetry comes to mind. Just last week we had a poetry contest for NHS...and,— I ask your indulgence, please, so I might share with you a few of the poems they submitted...

Many of them picked up on the Valentine's Day theme just a week ago:

1. Hearts & Flowers, Chocolate Candy, — I love you my Sugar-Plum Dandy!!...

And here's one obviously submitted by a student taking geometry, trigonometry, or calculus:

2. Now, I can count to seven, and I can count to nine, — But I would count forever if you'll be my Valentine!!...

Now, this one offers fair warning:

3. I'LL CRACK YOUR RIBS, I'LL BREAK YOUR SPINE, IF YOU WON'T BE MY VALENTINE !!! Love, Bubba...

And finally, one from the kid who obviously got the holidays mixed-up:

4. 'Tis the night of Halloween, — Won't You Be My Valenteen???!

Ah Yes! The adrenalin and anticipation are electric!! Who is the winner??

Prithee, Praytell & Forsooth?! The Envelope, please...

Alas, there's not a Robert Frost or Maya Angelou in the bunch.!!

• •

It is always my pleasure to be part of this NHS Induction Ceremony. I've been an honorary member since 1971...HONORARY member: Definition – He can spell National Honor Society. But, I wear my NHS pin with great pride and thanksgiving...Just a few words about the adults on the stage tonight. Dori MkNeel joins Shair Shure as NHS sponsor. She knew she was in for a task when Shair gave her the First Year Sponsor Kit — consisting of a whip, a chair, and a pistol!...and very much like Smith Barney, told Doris that in NHS we make money the old fashioned way...WE SELL CANDY!!! Every dentist on the beach will be your friend! Folks, we're talking Cavity City!!

From the administration, we welcome Chuk Skott, Assistant Principal For Community Schools, and, Layr Pawk, our principal. These guys are good!! They're all over campus with their walkie-talkies... which double as cattle prods. Gets them through the crowded halls REALLY fast! "ZAPP"! Or, if the kids are showing too much PDA (parents, you remember PDA – Public Display of Affection) a little too much Huggy Bear, or Smacky Mouth, then "ZAPP"! "Get To Class!" — Kid staggers away dazed — "WOW! SOME KISS! See ya fourth period !!!..."

My wife and children are bona fide members of NHS, and I'm hanging onto my honorary membership for dear life! But, isn't it interesting how these kids report their grades to their parents?? If

it's a "C", it's 'He GAVE me a "C"'. But if it's an "A", it's 'I MADE AN
"A"!…Aahhh, the perspective of youth.

And, finally, Jeannie Blaylock, news anchor from NBC's Channel 12.
Such an impressive list of credentials and major accomplishments:

1. One time she got all made-up to look like a Bag Lady to see
   what living on the street with the homeless was REALLY like.

2. In addition to that, she is the highly recognized founder of the
   Buddy Check Twelve Program which has done remarkable
   things in the field of breast cancer awareness and research
   throughout the United States, Canada, and other countries.

3. For Hurricane Katrina, Jeannie stood at ground zero with pho-
   tographers and reporters to conduct interviews with victims
   of the storm.

4. And, a while back, she returned to Vietnam, years after
   that terrible conflict, exploring the very same caves, trenches,
   and tunnels which were used for both attack and survival. She
   confided in me that the sub-title for that segment was HELL
   REVISITED!!…If she is not a special journalist, nobody is. So,
   what a pleasant task it must be for Ms. Blaylock to speak to
   Fletcher's chapter of NHS tonight. Fletcher is still one of the
   five best high schools with one of the best libraries in the
   county, and don't let anybody tell you different. Don't ever
   take your good brains for granted. TOOOO many kids, even
   kids whose parents love them as much as your parents love
   you, will NEVER see an "A", or "B" on their report card. You
   are in a very special group tonight. I congratulate you and
   wish you success in all your endeavors. Thank you for your
   indulgence, and now on with the good stuff. Without further
   adieu, please welcome, Ms. Jeannie Blaylock, and The Induction Ceremony to follow.

• •

Once again, it is my pleasure to take part in the NHS Induction
Ceremony. Such an impressive group of platform guests: Dr. Layr
Pawk, DUF Principal; Dr. Addam Hebert, President of UNF; Mr.

Frid Krysmun, Fletcher's Vice-Principal; ....and then there's me... Abdelnour...I can hear you wondering: Who's he??

Abdelnour...sounds like somebody they picked from the 'Rent-A-Teacher-That-Sounds-And-Looks-Like-An-Iraqi' pool. Actually, Layr Pawk and I were classmates at Andrew Jackson High School, and we were both working on our class re-union...only problem was we couldn't get enough of our classmates out on parole - am I right, Layr?

Dr. Hebert, it's always nice to have you here at Fletcher. You know, UNF's mascot is the osprey...a bird of prey like the eagle, hawk, owl, or falcon...Now, I'm not suggesting that he's here on a predatory mission, but he would certainly love to capture any of you to enroll at his school, now in its 33rd year. We're very proud of all the good Fletcher kids who go to The University of North Florida.

Frid Krysmun, if you read in the last issue of "The Northeaster", Fletcher's student newspaper has a more endearing name for him: ROBO-KRYSMUN!! "You are now eight seconds late for class... 40 LASHES WITH A WET PENCIL!!"

Then, there's you folks who just might take your good brains for granted. You, who are able to read, write, and count better than MOST of the kids in a comprehensive high school like Fletcher. And your good parents who are hard to con with your phony-baloney excuses to stay home and miss school: — My hair hurts! I'm dying from terminal hangnail! My teeth itch!! — Enough of my nonsense. This is a very special evening for you. May your curiosity and quest for knowledge never dim! And now, the inductees.

• •

One of my delightful functions of springtime is to induct the new members into the Fletcher chapter of NHS. NHS..."What does it mean?", I hear you ask. Well, different things to different people. To some of you at times worried about your precious GPA, it might have meant NEED HELP SOOOON!! And just look at the leadership and membership! Now, I know I promised them that I would not embarrass them tonight... but, I have been known to lie at times. But, they have also been picking on me, and in my own defense, I must set straight the reasons I was rejected from Bob Marley's Reggae Dance Troupe, as well as the Damascus Philharmonic... both in the same day...As to the first, it is difficult enough to dance when one has TWO left feet; alas, in my case, I have THREE! As to the second, the concertmaster informed me that they had already met their quota for kazooists... Sooo, have a little respect for your elders!

As your teachers, we never cease to be amazed at what a delightful joy, challenge, ...sometimes puzzlement... other times outright conflict!... and sometimes, a genuine pain in the whatchamcallit... it is to have you in our classes!! To wit: In addition to Sewanee (University of the South), the lovely Taira has also applied to Oxford, The Sorbonne, Scripps Institute of Oceanography, ...and to Lana's Center For Sandals and Macrame Fashions... Go figure.

I am also reminded of the recent gladiatorial 'Can You Top This' contest between our resident women's libber, and male chauvinist, Juili & Alix. In verse, they were to make their individual sexist points.

SHE was first:
   "Two & two are four, four & four are eight, –
   Being masculine's OK, but being FEMALE'S GREAT!!"

They ooh'd; They ahh'd; HE felt chagrin, but slowly recovered & responded:

"Two & two ARE four, four & six are ten, –
 You ladies came from Adam's Rib, and the Good Lord said AH-MEN!!"

   Touche'!   But, I digress...

• •

This time of year is induction time at Fletcher High School for the new members of NHS, that very special fraternity/sorority which is truly national in scope and an honorable society to be sure. My, my – such a diverse chapter we have. One of our more WASP-ish members is thoroughly convinced that there is obviously a conspiracy from the Islands of Mindanao and Luzon. He has counted, and sure enough -- there really are more Filipinos in Fletcher's NHS chapter than there are in Manila!!!

And parliamentarian Mikey is on the board not only for his good size (ya see, as parliamentarian, he also acts as sergeant-at-arms AND bouncer!), but also to prove that you do not have to have long hair, be Filipino, and speak Tagalog to be an officer in NHS!! Madam Prez simply likes the odds, 5:1 – and just loves snappin' orders to five good lookin' guys!

Some of our more restless scholars seem to have an aversion to going to class. Jennifer has asked on more than one occasion,--'Is 4th. period really necessary?' This is backed up by Mark, who wants to know if going to 3rd. period twice, will make up for going to 6th. period once. First period Jessie, though admitting it's a little early for snacks, wants all of you to know her two favorite pizza toppings are pine straw & feathers...Connivers, Allll!!

• •

SOCIAL STUDIES AWARD:

Having taken every social study offered at Fletcher, and audited each of them at least twice, – this year's recipient has now put together a new course to be offered next fall... Something about: The Social, Cultural, Political, and Psychological Ramifications and Mating Habits Evoked Upon Joining The Anopheles Mosquito and Monarch Butterfly – AND – has guaranteed a textbook for every caterpillar in the county. And, the recipient of the Social Studies Award this year is 'Sammy Social'!

• •

Once again, it is my annual sincere pleasure to take part in the NHS induction ceremony, (as for most of my years at Fletcher). The graduates are all going to various institutions of higher learning, ...if for no other reason than because their schools are located up in the mountains...(??).

Some of them have chosen some interesting schools to attend. One young lady spoke of going to OSU...thinking she was considering Oregon State, Oklahoma State, or Ohio State, I said: "Good for you! Best wishes!"…Well, it seems she was an expert in folding paper and chose to go to Origami Specialist University…(sigh…)

Until I learned that one young man had a keen interest in heart-shapes, daggers, anchors, dragons, ear lobes, eyebrows, belly buttons, and nipples, I was not sure what his choice of school was: IBPT – Institute of Body Piercing & Tattooing! (Where was THAT on the SAT??!!)

And, of course, there are always a few who want to impress you by using initials and acronyms: One young man told me he was headed for UCLA…WOW! University Common to Loquacious Androids. (…any bets as to its location?…)

A few were even more stultifying: CSBSD – Culinary School for Beauty School Dropouts; or, Lethargic Academy for Metaphysical Education, whose acronym, of course, is LAME; and, finally – College for Lobsters Of the Deep – CLOD. I should have known… She had two long antennae and pinched me on the, uh, – arm!

Sooo, Mom/Dad – don't think your money IS NOT being well spent — I will think it for you!!

• •

Seven schools competed! – One emerged victorious! Last night at the Fair Grounds, in the ABC Channel 25 Competiion, Fletcher's chapter of National Honor Society won first place, AND a brand new computer for the Mighty Purple! RAH!

Starting off with the cow-milking contest, 'Becca' "Squirt-Squirt" took second place for Fletcher! Good girl, 'Becca!

Next – The Big Foot Race: Fletcher placed third; Sooo, if you see Nicole, Brittany, and Karen holding ropes and walking funny, you'll know why…..

Tug-Of-War??…We're not going to talk about it…..

Then, in the final come-from-behind event of the Pie-Eating Contest, Brother and winner "Alka-David-Seltzer" consumed an entire chocolate cream pie in 2 minutes and 4 seconds!…….However,

David will not eat again until Thanksgiving Day…….

Yooda Man, David!!!

• •

Can you see this pin I'm wearing?…(lie to me…say YES!) Well, I've worn it with great pride for 32 of the 33 years I've been at Fletcher…I still remember dearly the folks in that class who inducted me into this chapter: Stephanie, Tommy, Mitzi.

People don't wear NHS apparel any more…don't want to come across as a braggart. We wear all sorts of caps, T-shirts, sweat shirts, and jerseys with pride… NBA, NFL, Fletcherettes, band, soccer team, Seminoles, Gators, Dolphins, and Buffy's Hang-Ten-Go-Get-'Em Surf Shop!! But NO! Not NHS! Don't want people to think that I think I'm smart!! Read, write, and count – gosh, a bunch of people can do that. BUT, To read AND heed, comprehend, retain, analyze, evaluate, investigate… To read AND write prose, poetry, drama, instruct, caution, report, praise, formula, recipe… To count AND calculate, compute, predict, forecast, temperature, weight, time, rate, distance… Believe me when I tell you folks, a countless number of kids would change places with you in a heartbeat!!

Don't ever take your good brains for granted; OR your good parents who pushed, shoved, pulled, cajoled, begged, pleaded, beat you with your textbooks to make sure you have achieved at this level. OR, your slave-driving teachers who brought you to near-death with assignments and homework and tests. If they didn't love you, they would not do any of those things. So, I offer a simple limerick before I call out your names for induction:

> To assure one a life of propriety,
> Performance is one of sobriety,
> Your senses ARE keener,
> You've a special demeanor,
> In the National Honor Society.

Whatever you do in this organization, I will take it personally. This is my chapter, just like it's your chapter, and I congratulate you with all sincerity.

• •

It is only fitting that we have such an outstanding platform of guests for this auspicious (or is that suspicious?) occasion. I know that many would agree with me that the reason Duncan U. Fletcher is the most successful chapter of NHS in Northeast Florida is because of Sponsor Haylin, a truly great and dedicated teacher.

And, no one is more deserving of being Teacher Of The Year than Miss Debre – How could she miss? She is one of my former students, AND I taught her all she knows!... right... I can spell calculus and still think it's something the dentist removes from your teeth!!... She truly is the best.

This annual function is always such an uplifting experience for me... (Gosh, that sounds like a bra commercial!) Let me re-phrase that, such a heart-warming experience... (STILL sounds like a bra commercial!)... I'll get it right yet!

To the new members, no sermon. Your induction is a commendable experience. Don't ever take it lightly. Countless kids are struggling daily just to make a C or D, let alone an A or B. I'm very proud of you and congratulate you sincerely.

• •

...Now, I'm not saying that all NHS'ers are bores and eggheads, but they are blessed. They are gifted. Most of them even realize how very fortunate they are for having the good brains and loving parents, plus the fortunate opportunities they have had to make it into NHS which requires so much more than simply having an inclination for academics.

Unfortunately, a few of them did NOT learn some of the simple lessons of life and were bounced out of the organization; the social graces DO apply. And, although they are not ALL eggheads, some of them need to lighten up a little, stop taking themselves so seriously, and lose that blasted 'Better-Than-Thou' attitude.

Chapter 12

Eggheads

...Advanced Placementally speaking, the high school programs intended for the college bound were usually saturated with those very same NHS students I so freely picked on earlier. Such a delight to have a classroom full of kids who were there because they WANTED to be there, instead of because they HAD to be there. To hear them tell it, ALL of the A.P. teachers were merciless, heartless, sarcastic, slave drivers. This is true – except that we all truly tried not to treat them as if ours was the only course they were taking. Those who were not really A.P. material were weeded out early in the school year. Otherwise, – not fair to them or the ones who could keep up with the tremendous work load.

Their just rewards are tossed back to them when at year's end, a very nice luncheon is given in their honor for those who took the absolutely skull-crushing A.P. Exams.

Egghead is a term reminiscent of the days when people had a difficult time placing a label on the likes of Adlai Stevenson, Gore Vidal, and William F. Buckley, Jr. and is not used very much in academic circles today. It stands for the academician; the smart, bright, scholarly type – sometimes – but not always, a nerd. So, conjure up your own very best mental image as we honor a few of the really accomplished students who took the very demanding A.P. courses in high school in preparation for going to college.

Here are some presentations awarded to a few of those who made it through my A.P. Psychology course.

• •

PRESENTATIONS: A.P. PSYCHOLOGY (A.P. Luncheon)

Just a word about the attitude of these folks who take A.P. Psychology:

They are not overjoyed, and sometimes annoyed –

By some super-shrink they call Sigmund Freud!

They even voted to change the name of the course from A.P. Psychology to A- Matter- Of- Gray- Matter. You must have seen them in the hall... All the guys stopping the 9th grade girls and asking them,

"Hey, Babe — Have you seen my new Freudian Couch???... Wanna try it out??"

• •

Our first award goes to Brother Rob Cordy, better known in my class as Sir Sleep-A-Lot!! Honestly, Rob has the uncanny ability to turn any desk, chair, table, locker, or classroom floor into a bed! And, I'm not sure that saying Rob snores loudly is accurate, HOWEVER, the last time he took a nap, the walls vibrated, and the U.S. Seismological Office pinpointed an epicenter of a class-eight earthquake right here at Fletcher High School with a reading of 97 on the Richter Scale! Rob Cordy, c'mon down, bubba!

• •

You know, a bunch of you could earn a trophy for inventing phony-baloney excuses: I met this very angry blue jay on my way to school, and no kidding... he really did steal my homework paper! OR, on the very unofficial Senior Skip Day: I was abducted by aliens...PUH-LEEZE!! OR, Hey Martha, can you write like my mother?? OR...Please excuse Freddy.... he has terminal criminal hangnail! OR, My teeth itch!!!

Well, Rys Kapps gets my vote and admiration for a most original excuse. You may or may not know that Rys is in the market for an airplane, and in particular, a CESSNA airplane. The other day he came in with a note that read: 'Please excuse Rys for being absent — he had a really bad case of CESSNA-ITIS!!' You win, Rys, and this flight's for you, Cap'n Kapps!

• •

If you ever see Bran Hydn and he's not smiling, you can bet that World War VI is upon us! Bran is pondering such funny issues as (1) How to watch paint dry, (2) The changing of the leaves, (3) Why are there freckles? And (4) the ever popular, molecular structure of The Number Nine. He really is a neat guy to be around and have in class, so come on up Mr. Smile-A-Mile, we love ya!

If it's about food, it's about Timm Lonard! To Timm, it doesn't have to be eggs....if it's edible, it's incredible!! And, you just have to wonder... WHERE DOES HE PUT IT ALL?? I mean, he must have hollow legs! Gosh, he's six feet tall, and still weighs 107 pounds! However, we do want to squash one terrible rumor about Timm... He wants to be sure you know that the restaurants at the beach are NOT going to change their signs from 'All You Can Eat' to 'All You Can Eat BEFORE TIMMY GETS HERE'!! Mr. Prez. — your award right here!!

• •

Well, we had to save our one lonely Junior until last. Lann Sallos is a very special young lady. She will be life-guarding at Hanna Park this summer, and YES FELLAS, it is still against the law to fake a drowning just so Lann will come to the rescue!! We had a lot of fun picking on her this year, and we love her dearly. So, come on up Super-Psycho Swimmer!!

That wraps it up for me, folks and I thank you for your indulgence.

• •

...Now, I'm not saying that I brag too much about the caliber of kids who come through Fletcher's A.P. Program, but I probably brag too much about... O.K., I do. But, when you have students who consistently make 4's & 5's on A.P. U.S. History, Calculus, Physics, Language Arts, and my personal favorites of European History and Psychology – you can't help but be proud.

• •

When you've had students make it into every university of the Ivy League, ACC, SEC, Cal Tech, Stanford, University of the South — Sewanee, TN, Chicago, Big Ten, MIT, Military Academies, and even a few into Oxford, Heidelberg, Bologna, Madrid, and The Sorbonne, and countless others — you can't help but be proud. (Did I mention the caliber of Fletcher's Advanced Placement program?...)

Chapter 13

Presentations

...Teacher/Faculty/Mentor/Instructorally speaking, my fellow colleagues never seem to escape my abuse. I pick on them 24-7 as I have for 33 years at Fletcher High School. They are such good sports, and STOP feeling sorry for them, for goodness sake! They all retaliate with precision and gusto! As a matter of fact, I have been on the defensive/receiving end of countless barbs for which I had NO response! It's just the nature of the rapid-fire repartee we all need and enjoy as part of our way to cope and maintain our sanity in this very complicated endeavor we call the Ed. Biz.

We, too, are rewarded at year's end with a very nice banquet, and, of course, more verbal darts. Witness the following:

• •

PRESENTATIONS: TEACHERS END OF YEAR DINNER PARTY

How fortunate for Fletcher to be a coastal high school. It is part of the reason that our marine biology program is top notch under the leadership of Gairy-The-Teach.

1. Remember last year every time we saw Gairy he had his hands pointing upward like a just-scrubbed surgeon? Of course, instead of rubber gloves he was wearing bandages up to his elbows. It seems Gairy just cannot keep his hands to himself, and sometimes, mother nature fights back (or should I say, bites back?) And, so for his perseverance and success, we present to him the Moray Eel Award, for having gone one whole semester without being bitten by an eel, shark, or student! C'mon up, Gair!

2. You don't ever want to make fun of her name (or accent) — rumor has it that she is able to turn you into a quadratic equation if you do!! The recipient for the Coolest First Name Award is, (who else?) Nnngongama Majose!!

3. On any given morning, or any given weather, with clipboards in hand, there they are on their assigned posts — Eli and Jim are on Bus Duty, and although the students still refer to the great Yellow Hounds as Fletcher State Prison Vehicles, these two stalwarts are most deserving of the 'Bus Drivers Are Your

Friends' award. Advance, Stalwarts!

4. Tim has finally taught his whole department that all things contain carbon and that Avogadro's Law has absolutely nothing to do with Mafia Justice...Timothy, you are the winner of the Mr. Wizard Award.!!

5. Notice how the tone of the memos from curriculum got a little more ominous as the year progressed?! That's because the 'Thank You For Your Usual Co-operation' Award goes to Jozie, our Queen of Curriculum!

6. At times, some students are misplaced in a course far over their head. At times, whip-cracking Haylin was not quite sure if she should teach them or water them! 'GROW LITTLE FUNGUS'!! She does, however, change the sawdust in her classroom between periods...Ms. Haylin, winner of the 'Who Put This Kid In My A.P. Class?!' Award.

7. Debre Lynn: Math Teacher Extraordinaire: "Yes, I DO know that calculus is a deposit which forms on one's teeth, but not in THIS class! You want dentistry, dial 1-800-FILLING!" Go get 'em, Deb! You are the winner of the 'Don't Tell Me Your Troubles' Award!!

8. Who Am I??: 'What? Only six classes, two languages and four other preps? Gosh! Maybe I can teach Latin and Greek NINE PERIODS/DAY next year!... I sure hope so!...' And the 'Glutton For Punishment' award goes to...Liz G.!!

9. Ever have a seventh period from Hell? Yeah, I've had 'em. Rich told me he had a kid so impossible he did not know which of the following applied: This kid (A) was as big as a truck (B) could bench press a truck (C) is a truck (D) ate a truck. In good faith, I think he can make good on his quest: 'If I Could Talk To The Animals In My Seventh Period!...' Rich Silbus, come on up...you are most deserving of the 'Dr. Doolittle' Award!

10. Whether he's in jeans, shorts, or Brooks Brothers suit, Kev wears a tie. Strange...he hates neckties, and when Brenna

said, 'Kev, we're going to the Faculty Party', Kev said, 'Aw! Friday Night?' Right now he's glaring at her saying: 'Gosh, I could be home now watching the Red Sox/Yankees game! Kev, you are one of my former students, you are crazy, and you win the 'I Hate Neckties' Award!

11. And finally, we have the 'Instant Justice' OR the 'We Don't Need Your Kind Round Here' Award. Not being much of a surfer, Koop's answer to juvenile crime would be to give a more literal interpretation to the concept of Hang Ten! Typical Townie! C'mon up, Koop.... U R The Best!!

Thanks, Folks. I had a good time. I hope you did.

• •

...Now, I'm not saying one must have a thick skin to survive the rigors of too many friendly jabs on our faculty, but it just might help if one of your parents is an elephant, tapir, hippo, rhino, porcupine, or suit of armor. That's why Faculty Follies was such a good time. We poked fun at almost everybody we knew (or thought we knew) could take a joke, and sometimes we gambled...and LOST! (Remind me to check next time to see if that guy's mother really was related to Attila the Hun! All slander and libel lawsuits on the spindle, please.)

Chapter 14

Jeopardy

...Hyperbolically speaking, there seems to be no limit as to those inane activities one deems necessary to perform, or to those who delight in judging those activities as if they were worthy of any assessment whatsoever...(?) (If you have ANY idea of what I just said, PLEASE notify me because I don't have the foggiest!) Anyway, part of the nonsense we conducted in our efforts to make the kids laugh and earn a few bucks for our extracurricular endeavors was a parody we performed in a somewhat twisted version of 'JEOPARDY!' Our panel of judges consisted of both students and faculty whom we visit at the Funny Farm the second Wednesday of every week. If anyone is still left standing after this bomb, please remember – we're just a stone's throw away from Mayo Clinic.

• •

But, hearten, oh ye of little faith. Thinkest thou for one iota that we would leave decisions of such import to whimsy or chance?? NAY! SAY DURST!!

Merv Griffin, Alex Trebek, John O'Hurley, Pat Sajak, and all the powers that be – please, invoke thine influence to all the game show gods, to please, PLEASE CUT US SOME SLACK!! PLEEZ!

• •

JEOPARDY (FOR SURE)!

Against our better judgement, we had a Family Feud/Jeopardy-like contest between our illustrious language arts department (still trying to convince all of us to call the library a 'media center'...), and science department faculties. Their responses were interesting, to say the least...well, less than least, actually. You be the judge.

We conducted a survey of 100 seniors: Which new foods would you like to see on Fletcher's cafeteria menu?

LANGUAGE ARTS:

Player #1 Carla Composition
Lizzard Salad...

Player #3 Priscilla Participle
Ptomaine Tarts!

Player #5 Samantha Spellwell
Not-So-Mysterious-Meat

Player #7 Vickie The Verb
Sautéed Alligator Toes

SCIENCE:

Player #2 Zoe Ology
Peanut Butter & Tree
Bark Sandwiches

Player #4 Anna Tomy
Real Food?

Player #6 Lillie Lepidoptera
Steamed Oyster Shell

(Gosh! And for this I gave up Bowling for Broccoli!)

Player #8 Freddie Fizzix
Bread & Water

NOW, JUST IN CASE YOU HAVEN'T FIGURED OUT THAT IT WAS TRULY A LESSON IN FUTILITY, CHECK OUT GAME #2. IT DID NOT GET BETTER:

We conducted a survey of 100 underclassmen:Which new courses would you like to see added to Fletcher's curriculum?:

Carla-   How to find a
restroom that's
open after 2:45!!

Zoe-   Surfing for anyone
but TOWNIES!

(Good Grief! There's wrestling at the Coliseum tonight!
What AM I doing here??!))

Priscilla- SEXOLOGY...
WITH LAB! (Hmm...)

Anna-   Basic Hall-Pass
Forging...

(GUIDANCE PROMISED ME THAT WE'D
BE USING LIVE PEOPLE TONIGHT!)

Samantha- Elementary
Vandalism...

Lillie-   ADVANCED
Vandalism!

Vickie-   Anatomy By
Braille (Hmm...)

Freddie-   Anything You Ever
Wanted To Know
About Freddie But
Were Afraid To Ask

We employed the wisdom of several top notch graduating seniors, PLUS, the experience of several members of our great faculty to help us with such academic issues. Please meet them now:

SENIORS:

- Keeping in shape while still pondering whether to pass up his last eight years of college eligibility, or go straight to the Pros, our first judge still holds the record for bench-pressing seven sophomores in the cafeteria at lunchtime. Who else but Steve Rylle?

- He's called the alchemist of grade-switching for persistence in his countless efforts in trying to talk teachers into a higher letter grade ('but I didn't KNOW about the da-da-ra'). A warm welcome for Pete Yolds.

- Probably not a first round draft choice for the NBA, this judge just finished her whirlwind tour of all Pygmy villages in Africa, and signing autographs on her latest book entitled 'Thinking And Living Short', by golly, here she is, Jocelyn Neemo.

- More than willing to judge The Follies, this next fellow was determined to be here tonight to prove to all that YES, his hair DOES glow in the dark and he has more volume decibels than any Dolby Sound System, we all know him as Rogie Feeld!

- Having recently conducted the new popular workshop for Senior High School Club Officers, "37 Excuses For Not Attending Club Board Meetings", say hello to Lita Sasson.

- Adding to her already impressive list of pageant victories, we welcome tonight the winner of her latest competition, 'Miss Huckleberry Pie Festival', all the way from Lizard Breath, Wisconsin, Mary Anrigg.

Special thanks for our voluntary student consultants who graciously agreed to assist their classmates in their judgmental duties:

- The weekend warriors of Kevin, Kevin, & Chuck (Larry, Curly, and Moe) who will also conduct a seminar at Hanna Park on what to do with that mysterious extra sleeping bag before Mom & Dad start asking questions...

- And Dan Krew, in his four-time effort to grow a respectable beard by the time he hits the JU campus next fall, has relinquished all his Gillette and Schick razors to Tom Meeed, the ONLY man in the Senior Class able to grow a daily five o'clock shadow by 9:30 in the morning --- ANY morning!

(If I hurry, I can still make it home for the Martha Stewart television documentary — Twenty-Seven Things To Do With Used Dental Floss!)

FACULTY:

- Taking time out from his teaching duties, and busy schedule of endorsing every major athletic shoe company in Sopchoppy, Florida, please welcome Mark Potters

- Having earned a well deserved break from her very profitable avocation as CEO of her Designer Parachute Boot Enterprise, our First Lady of Fashion, Ms. Barbara Teer.

- Just back from a whirlwind tour of a day and three hours reviewing the top night spots in Ypsilanti, Michigan, The Titanic of Talent Scouts, Ms. Sara Osbo.

- And finally, from her active desk as chief editor of that brilliant documentary, Fifty-Five Things To Do With Obsolete Brain Brawl Questions, the scholarly and lovely Ms. Haylin Furnezz.

Our sincere thanks to all our student and faculty judges...(on 3rd. thought, just skip the previous three pages and continue reading...)

• •

...Now, I'm not saying that at this point we have totally lost it, but — I think at this point — Gosh, YES — we HAVE totally lost it! Television's 'Jeopardy' may have just been dealt a blow from which it might not fully recover, or ever want to! If it goes to trial, here's hoping that Perry Mason or Ben Matlock will take our case, gratis, pro bono, FREE!: 'I'll take Cube-Shaped Ball Bearings for $9.12, Alex...'

Chapter 15

Faculty Follies

...Aerodynamically speaking, the bumblebee cannot fly (sounds familiar, right?). His body is too large and heavy for his wings to carry him aloft. The bumble bee, however, does not know this, and like the 'Little Engine That Could', musters up determination enough, and rises to the occasion! And, 'VOILA'!! The bumble bee CAN and DOES indeed FLY!!

People are not always blessed with such resolve. Witness some of the trials, tribulations, and foibles of personalities galore, which, I am sure you will recognize in one form or another.

For years, one Bill Abdelnour was the scourge of the faculty at Duncan U. Fletcher Senior High School, Jacksonville Beach, Florida. Why? Because he never took NO for an answer in recruiting and drafting every teacher and staff member on the faculty to participate in an annual spring fling known as Fletcher Faculty Follies. Yes, I DO realize that not everyone has a talent, knack, or nerve enough to get up in front of an audience and act silly or straight for five minutes. Still, I was a bully and badgered them annually and mercilessly all the way to the spotlight on stage. Most (heavy on the most) of them thanked me later for forcing them to have a good time, letting their hair down, and letting their students have a good laugh at their expense, and earning a few bucks [from time to time] for the Senior Class or National Honor Society.

Here are some of the tactics of promotion I used to have the Faculty Follies Show become a reality for nearly twenty years. Following are some of the fliers I placed in every teacher's mailbox to get them to start thinking (good or evil) about the Big Teacher 'Talent' Show. The reactions often varied from 'Way to go, Bill!' to 'Oh! NO! NOT AGAIN!'

• •

Hiya Teach! Say, do ya have any talent?? Gosh, I sure hope not! 'Cuz if you do, you don't qualify for the Senior Class Annual Fletcher Faculty Follies Show!! Yeah Teach, we want every single (married, divorced, widowed, living-in-sin, human) adult on our staff to take part in this production, AND your classes deserve a chance to see you in action**. (**Translation: make a complete spectacle of yourself).

Please check any of the following items you would be willing (or unwilling) to try for the show:

1. Sing, dance, musical instrument, dramatic reading...(boring!)...

2. Imitate a sandspur...

3. Chew gum & breathe simultaneously...

4. A 3-minute graphic interpretation of "Gone With the Wind" painted with my left foot...

5. Donate my body for whatever you see fit...(pretty kinky, eh?!)

6. Face in the crowd (3, 29, 106)...

7. 'I'm not going to try it. Let's get Mikey to try it!'

8. I'm too talented & do not qualify...

9. Sumtheeng orijynul...

10. Your name please...

...Now prepping for our annual normal (or abnormal) bout with sanity, the Senior Class once again plans for the Fourth Annual Faculty Follies Show...NO! PLEASE!! NOT THE CIRCULAR FILE!! (WOW! THAT WAS CLOSE!). So far we have firm commitments from the following:

- Barnhorst – a closetbassoonist..(or is that a bassoonet closetist?).

- Koviak & Fawstir – sing an aria from "Madame Butterfly" in Swahili…

- Tem Alyn will rap his own original version of that ever popular teacher tune: *I Found Happiness When I Levitated The Dumbest Kid In My Class Right Through The Brick Wall Proving Once Again That Newton Was Wrong And That There REALLY IS A Fifth Dimension:"*

You can't lose! This year's theme is wide open – Fletcher's Faculty Fantasy. ALMOST anything 'Penthouse' would NOT print will be welcome.

You can and will: sing...dance…do impressions (ostrich, Martian, guacamole, coffee pot, amoeba, Tee-shirt, stage prop, other), play the sitar, kazoo, radio, or musical saw...In any case, don't MAKE me come after you!

(ABDELNOUR, you never give up, do you!?)

We love you, Fabulous Faculty!

• •

OK!! ALL RIGHT!! – So you have 72 other things to do already – So What?? Big Deal! Who Cares??? Just tell me what you're going to do for the 5th. annual Fletcher Faculty Follies Show, Tuesday, March 29 (date subject to change...so, what else is new??)

FIRM COMMITMENTS SO FAR:

- Jaf Haylit – a performance from his latest work: "Ballet In A Conch Shell" (yawn).

- Holli Moover – types a 4-minute dissertation on the joys of teaching comatose kids while keeping time to the music of John Philip Sousa's "Billie Jean". (that's really good, Holl!)

- Sym Dysh impersonates a howitzer shell fired from a pea shooter into a damp tea bag (proud of you, Sym!)

It's our half-decade anniversary!! We need your participation!! A few suggestions? SURE!:

Impressions: gerbil, pencil, oatmeal, bean sprout, pewter mug, OR, ... (Abdelnour, will you just stow it, please?!)

Ye Olde Great Faculty! Abdel....

• •

UNDAUNTED (last year the Abdel-man was daunted as cries of "SACS STUFF" rang through his ears.) Ah, yes – SACS...The Southern Association of Colleges & Schools...came to us for their dreaded (at least, to teachers) evaluation visit to make sure we were still an accredited comprehensive high school. We were. He pursued his goal of celebrating the (almost 6th.) anniversary of the FACULTY FOLLIES!! Confident that he would not hear any such references to SACS, SACKS, SAX, SACKETTES, or CAQUES. He asked the faculty and staff to inform him of their many talents they would perform in the show this year.

Early returnees show just a few examples of the extraordinary abilities of our crew:

- Maru Hoolin – demonstrates her new computer technique of compressing three obnoxious kids into one neat compact, floppy disc (or cube)...(gets MY vote!)

- Dez Humiltone – trained his baseball team to lay their bodies prone on stage to spell out the word K-O-A-C-H!...(Well, Dezmond doesn't get out very much...

- And Lezlee (Patience-Of-Job) Kaler – conducts her 7th period class in an original recitation entitled "Middle East Muddler", the first titillating couplet of which goes:

> "At the risk of being slashed by a Savarin Sword,
> To the Ayatollah we present
> ...Freedom Of The Press Award!" (Brave lady, Lezlee!)

Show Time is April 25, or July 41 – whichever comes third.

Sure, Bill!! Count me in to impersonate a mastodon, kite, chalk eraser, electron.

Incidentally, unless you return this form in 9 & 12/7 minutes, it will self destruct, AND your classroom will be surrounded by kumquats! Don't take that chance!

• •

Dearly Beloved (or Barely Tolerable), The Senior Class proudly presents (or modestly invokes your indulgence for) the 7th annual Fletcher Faculty Follies Show!!... OK, so what? — SOOO WHAAAT?! Well, you are in the show, that's what!! (and yes, that is what you call your basic Democracy in Action). We have doubled the ticket price to $2.00!! Talk about a feeling of accomplishment.Well,...don't.

Your enthusiasm is already overwhelming!! So far, the following unsolicited volunteers have come forth to offer their talents:

- Rahja Woody is working diligently to include some new animals in his great mimic-menagerie. So far, he has perfected the Amorous Armadillo, Pterrible Pterodactyl, and the Killer Koala Bear...OK Rahj!!

- Mykal O'Stryker will prove the validity of the test scores (and divulge her true feelings) as she administers her own 2-minute version of the SSAT (Sophomore Students Are Troglodytes)... Well, Mykal is expressive at times...

- And Den Kulbri, yes, Fletcher's very own Wizard of Ooze (or is that Odds?) will demonstrate the first five chapters of his latest 'How To' book, Surfing In A Thimble... Let's, uh, hear it for Den.

Don't Dawdle!! Show Time is set for Tuesday, April 17...give or take a season. Almost Anything Goes! (as in your name GOES here.........!)

Gosh Bill, I've always had a burning desire to Pantomime/ Lip Sync/Kitchen Sink...Monologue/Dialogue/Hollow Log... Juggle/Jiggle/Giggle...Soft Shoe/Hard Shoe/Horse Shoe... Impersonate a(n) Sloth...Igloo...Nail...Thistle...Nano-Second...Or Something..............

• •

YAWL! (AKA You All, All Y'all, U-Haul, You-Uns, Youse guys)!

Now, don't even start with me with the....ah za za SACS....ah za za BLOCK SCHEDULE...ah za za SIX PERIOD DAY...ah za za NEW PRINCIPAL...ah za za SURPLUS TEACHER UNITS/REDUCTION IN STAFF...ahh...za...za...

FACT IS NOBODY GIVES A FLIP!! Just tell me what you plan to do in the Faculty Follies this year, Thursday, April 15...(Tax deadline has been moved to July 37).

• •

Kudos to these early (and courageous) participants:

- Jehr ("Being A Teacher Is Aardvark") Hairston will explain some of the shortcuts in his latest owner's manual – Raising Aardvarks For Fun & Profit (Jehr, you really need to consider latch hook).

- Chuk Skott will demonstrate his technique of burying chameleons (as well as the Geico Gecko and the Budweiser Iguana) in the atrium to guarantee posterity a future supply of fossil fuel. (Bless his conservationist heart).

- Maree Jardeau, still trying to decide if her latest opera should be entitled "Aeneid Re-visited", "Aeneas Was A Wimp", or "Forum Here To Eternity", will sing her most famous aria from that opera, "I'll Never Go Out With Vergil Again – His Hands Were Always Roman"! Maree, U R The Goodest!!

- Han Dolloway, in a Protean effort to extend the message that the Foreign Languages are alive and well, will impromptu live-and-on-stage…translate the Dead Sea Scrolls into Kechni, Swahili, and Tagalog, OR conjugate the verb to discombobulate in Sanskrit, Yiddish, and Choctaw…'Sehr Gut, Mein Freund'!

- And, Karl Jansi…using only a chair, a candle, and an inflatable doll will spoonerismically re-enact the entire balcony scene from "Romeo and Juliet!" GOU YO, JARL KANSI!!

WILLIAM! Sign me up NOW to do the following:

— Warble	Impersonate:
(or Yodel, if you're Swiss)…	— plutonium
— Obey Terpischore (5, 6, 7, 8)	— bubble
— Skit, Knit, Brad-a-Pitt...	— thumb print
— Play Hooky...(Just Kidding!)	— pollen
— Clog, Jog, Lost in Fog...	— chlorphyll
— Clap-Clap, Do a Rap...	— pentagon
(DON'T EVEN!)	— Madagascar
— Pole Vault, Somersault,	— enzyme
Pass the Salt...	

ORR, YOAR CHOYCE: _____ YOAR NAIM:_____

Well, you have OBVIOUSLY mistaken me for someone who believes: 'G Byll…aye mustavv mysplayst myy Phakultee Pholleez Phorm…'

But you are WRONG Pencil Pusher!!

FIND IT <u>NOW!</u> FILL IT IN <u>NOW!</u> TURN IT IN <u>NOW!</u>…(or an evil spirit will befall you…and may the fleas of 12,000 camels nestle in your hair!

• •

OK TEACH. You probably think I am a man of infinite patience… or that I will simply let it slide…WOE UNTO THEE AND THINE MISCONCEPTION! Twenty-nine teachers have signed up for the show, either written or verbally. Some of them even have something to DO in the show! Sooo, turn it on, up, and in! Otherwise, who knows WHAT might happen to your car tires?? And, besides, two new enforcers are now in my employ. You don't want to mess with them. Their names are Guido and Bubba…

Need I say more??

    Yo Evah Lovin' Syrian Soothsayer, Bill Abdelnour

• •

TU: Awl Fakultee 'n Staph

FRUM: Byll Abdelsomething

RHEE: Phakooltey Pholleez

So, just what qualifies you to participate in the Seventh (?) (keep your fingers crossed) Annual Fletcher Faculty Follies?? Absolutely ZIPPO!

Just (don't ya just hate offers that begin with JUST?) write your name on this form and tell me what you will be doing in the show this year. That's it! You win! And so do the kids who will pay to see you cut loose on stage and have a good time. So, c'mon, teach — this is not astrophysics, brain surgery, or income tax – YOU CAN DO THIS! Talent? What Talent?? It's the only 'talent' show in captivity for which having talent is irrelevant and a total detriment. Just (there it is again) check out our eager beavers who have already signed up:

Risko Cyd will tell us what he REALLY means by lexicographically illustrating his own definitions of two of his favorite acronyms – RHETORIC & AMBIANCE:

(Noah, Webster, LOOK OUT!!)

Red	Another
Hot	Mediocre
Educator	Bilateral
Tepid	Idea
On	And
Relegated	No
Input	Cigar
Concerns	Expected

- Li Phagun and Cher McDunn, yes, Fletcher's very own Mothers Earth, will match their teams – Phagun's Phelons VS. McDunn's Marauders – in that latest game show craze, CACF4 (Confiscate ALLLL Containers From Fast Food Franchises), the winning team earning a free trip to the South Pole for a chance to plug up the hole in the ozone layer over Antarctica, AND -- teach the penguins the latest dance craze – The Stompin' Styrofoam Shuffle!!

(Popsicle, Fudgsicle, Icicle, Bicycle,
I Cycle, You Cycle, We Cycle, Recycle)

- And, Rykk Jonnz, the original "G.I. Jonnz", will demonstrate the true meaning of patriotism by sending a score of unpatriotic students to the gallows simultaneously for not knowing how to field strip a ciggy &/or not being able to assemble an AK-47 in 2.2 minutes flat in total darkness. (NUKE 'EM, TOWNIE!)

BILL! I CAN HARDLY WAIT TO: Sing, Dance, Skit, Pantomime/ Commit a Crime, STRANGLE YOU!!...Impersonate a(n) Antonym... Bauble...Quilt...Placebo...Laser Beam...Kewpie Doll...Shucks, Bill...I can do something a whole lot more creative that ANY of these...

If you put this form down before you fill it in & return it to me, you will (1)Get Warts, (2)Lose Your Thumbs, AND (3)Get Thumbs & Lose Your Warts!!!

Teach-A-Rama!! Rejoice And Be Exceedingly Glad! – We are having a REVIVAL!!

SAY YAY-US!! A Revival of the Faculty Follies!...(What?) Get AWAY from that trash can! Shame on you! If you have any talent, you don't qualify anyway! So listen:

In the feel-good spirit of springtime fun, the following have ALREADY signed up to perform:

• Coaches Rik Benk and Sozy Wyatt will miniaturize the entire aquatic team, and while on stage, conduct the world's first Swim Meet In A Beer Mug!! Rich, Rik!! Go for it Soz!

• Holli Moover will finally let Fabio down easily, by singing to him the ever gentle "How Could You Believe Me When I Said I Loved You When You Know I've Been A Liar All My Life?!" Atta girl, Holl!

• Tomm LaMoynt, using only a Pez dispenser and a two-speed fan, will create a storm surge force SOOO powerful, the American Meteorological Society will label it Hurricane Zelda Armageddon. Tomm will forever thereafter be known as Mr. Blizzard...Oh, all right...DR. Blizzard! Good Stuff, Tomm!!

• And, Nngngama Mujov-Ceonn will perform a most unique interpretation of Alice Walker's masterpiece on stage as she uses only a triangular ruler to bludgeon some really bad kid with such ferocity, that he will actually turn "The Color Purple"— Great Fletcher Spirit, Gama!...(and all the Fletcher Faithful did wear their purple colors with pride.)

So, Rahj, muster up the menagerie; High Steppers, step higher; Bette, motivate Mortimer; Zee-Zee Toppp, start toppin'; Swinny Bopp, start boppin'!!

Byll, I will, I WYLL: Entertain the troops by — Reciting The Code Of Conduct!! (puh-leez...!)...Strip, Flip, Micro-Chip...Impersonate

a(n)   clothes   pin...quasar...virus...equal   sign...toothbrush...
paramecium...brick...comma...other...

• •

All proceeds go to scholarships...Oh, yes – and to compensate
our only paid professional, special guest appearance featuring the
ever lovable, "Harry Armz & The Folly-cles"!

AUFHÖREN! WARNING! MESSAGE! CAUTION! HALT! LISTEN! CO

D BALUK! ACHTUNG!

MPRENDE! ESCUCHEN!

> Now, - raise your hand if you thought (or at least hoped)
> Faculty Follies was on hiatus...Prithee! Pray Tell!
> Forsooth & Gadzooks (Boy/Girl) Wonder!
> Pencil-Pushin' Caped Crusader(ette)!!!
> YOU ARE RONG! RAWNG! WRONNGG!!

¡VERSTEHEN! HEED! LOOK! STOP! ¡ATTENCION! BULLETIN! DEER

We're talkin' your basic Fabulous Fletcher Follies Show, Fellow Facultyites, and we're off to a great start already with these brave signees:

- Using only four thumb tacks and two rubber bands, Myk Laveen will construct a utilitarian bridge from the main building to the auditorium so that on rainy days we can safely traverse that Slough of Despond and STILL remain un-wetted! (Gosh...You science guys...Such a marvel!)

- Klawdy Marshyl will demonstrate live on stage her own version of the Napoleonic Code of Hammurabi (??) in response to a kid who has no pencil by inserting an 8-inch rod of graphite into his left ear, and screaming "Hey Kid, – Sharpen This!" – Klawdy, You Go, Girl!

- And, Bil Doetee, still smarting from having been snubbed by the Roller Blade Corporation, will show us his ORIGINAL prototype for in-line skates...(of course, it just might be that the wheels on his first model of in-lines ran from side-to-side rather than from toe-to-heel...) Fret not, Brother Bill, & remember... they laughed at Edison!!

Sooooo, get your trusty pencil and check one of the following:

Geee Byll, hoo kn rezyst yorr nthuziazm?! And like the 'Little Engine That Could', I will:

— Sing, Fling, Pong-a-Ping — Dance, Prance, Try Romance — Skit, Flit, Be a Twit...Trombone, Saxophone, Chicken Bone...Recite a poem by Dr. Seuss (or eat six pounds of deep-fried moose....) WOW!...

Serious reading of a "Hamlet" sililoquy (zzz...) or impersonate (yawn) a(n):

— Bowl of Soup   — Mosquito Bite   — Finian's Rainbow
— Button   — Hall Pass   — Guillotine
— Ink Stain   — Feather   — Other

   Our special guest performance will be the smash hit song, "I'll See You In The Spring, If I Can Get Through The Mattress" by Billy & the Bedbugs! Sooo, Follies of the World, Unite!! You Have Nothing To Lose But Your Dignity! Alka-Seltzer said it best: 'Try It – You'll Like It!'

   This form is due back to me 12 minutes ago....or SOONER!

   Abdelnour,...(your favorite camel jockey...)

• •

HARK! PRITHEE! PRAY-TELL! FORSOOTH & GADZOOKS! FROM WHENCE HENCEFORTH IT COME! AMEN!...(and if that makes ANY sense to you, then YOU CANNOT be in the Faculty Follies Show this year!!) Yes, folks – can ya believe it's been a year already???... {what do you MEAN it seems more like a day & a half??! Shame on you!} So, mark your calendar. And, as usual, the 'I-Can-Hardly-Wait-Bunch' has already responded:

- Glyn Kuper, our very own Resident-First-Lady-Of-Clay, will perform a live demo on how NOT to mix-up students and pottery. She finally got it right: TEACH KIDS – PLACE POTTERY IN KILN! After all, we have all nearly forgotten that one little reversal last year. (Bless Her Ceramic Soul!)

- Sweet Suze Harrmonn will graphically prove once and for all that ONOMATOPOEIA is not spelled using all five vowels (and sometimes 'y'), by thumping it out in Morse Code, letter-by-letter, on the heads of a dozen kids using only two rubber mallets and a trampoline. (Harrmonn Hones In On Hard-Heads!)

- Jorj Paww will debut his new wrestling team –Those Wonderful Wizards Of Whump – and demonstrate new release techniques from these holds: Grendl – Grip Flying Wishbone Leg Scissors Whip – (bite opponent's shoulder, and yes, it is a new twist on the Mike Tyson Ear Cannibal Crunch); Figure-Eight Arm Twist – (ram ice-pick into opponent's left eye...works every time); and the Head-Lock Full Nelson Vice Device – (shoot opponent with pistol – SEE ICE-PICK RESULT). So, what do you think? Is He A Grappler's Delight, or what?!

- And, Steev Ortee and Mick Phogg will give us a quick preview of the latest dance sensations soon to be seen at this year's Prom: Ortee & The Oddballs team up with that newest rage – Priscilla & The Prom-Prom Girls; while Brother Phogg will show us the choreographic skills he learned from Fast-Foot Flora, as his troupe shows off with

'I Dance, You Dance,
We Dance, Guy-Dance'...
(Gosh, if only Fred Astaire could see them now...!)

So, don't even PRETEND you're not in the show...U-R! Just do what I tell ya! Phyll Yn Phorm Noww!! Geee Bylll! I Can Hardly Wait to join the 'I-Can-Hardly-Wait-Bunch'!! I WILL:
Bill, I plan to:

Seeeeeng _____ Mime-A-Dime-A-Crime:_____Impersonate A:
Dannss _____ Paint-Quaint-Taint-Faint _____
Skytt _____ Stripe _____ Color _____
Perform Acupuncture On A Porcupine (stalwarts only) _____
Garbanzo Bean _____ Corpuscle_____ Glitch_____
Other_____

This paper will not allow you to let go of it until you sign your name HERE _____NOW!

(The Athenians would have been so proud of me! Demos! Kratos!)
Billy Boy Abdelnour (NHS)

...And, especially for those teachers who just might be vexillologi-cally challenged, just so you'll know, we all fly the same flag: RAH! RAH! SIS! BOOM! BAH! Go get 'em Purple!! AND, in answer to a steadily diminishing number of requests (alas & anon), Fletcher Faculty Follies are upon us once more! Don't even THINK about turning down 'The Old Man' – it's probably his last hoorah!...Oh, just stop all that cheering and toasting,- you know you're going to miss me!...(I hope).

At the vanguard of this year's early entries are the following Captains Courageous:

• Karin Carin Cairyn Kairin Carren (gosh...talk about a repeat-ing decimal!...) will demonstrate her team's craft by venom-ously, vindictively, & voraciously, victimizing, vaporizing, & vanquishing those vexatious vixens, varmints, & vermin which versus her very vocal, valorous, & victorious volleyball volunteers!!...(and NO! I CANNOT say that three times fast!) DIG! SPIKE! KILL! YOODA GIRL, KC!!

• Nan Murzak will prove once and for all that Pythagoras and Euclid were WRONG!...that with benefit of camera, protrac-tor, calipers, and slide rule (a 1957 mechanical computer) show that some kids ARE born with heads that resemble obtuse, scalene, &/or isosceles triangles (depending on whether they are walking toward you or away from you)! Bless her obliquely arithmetical heart!!

- And, Ric Silbus will, in four minutes flat, concoct a soliloquy incorporating the drama of William Shakespeare, poetry of Robert Frost, eloquence of Sydney Lanier, sarcasm of William F. Buckley, Jr., and Pulitzer Prize winning one-liners from Alfred E. Neumann, such as: 'What? Me Worry?!' (Ric let it slip that his first line is a doozey! Something about: 'That light in yonder window shines...it's a CANDLE! YOU'RE ABOUT TO BURN DOWN THE HOUSE! YOU IDIOT!!). Ahh, yes, the razor-sharp, silver-tongued, silver-haired Silbus! (...fershlugginer & potzrebie...)

The Abdel-man is NOT famous for his patience,...soooo, what's it gonna be? Volunteer willingly? OR, a 12-year siege of your house by locusts and camels?!

OH! BILL! You Persuasive Person! I will do the following for Faculty Follies:

— Rub-a-dub-dub, drown you in a tub!

— Mimic & mime, & not charge a dime!

— Be Jack Nimble, & surf in a thimble!

— Imitate a quagga (-an extinct zebra-like mammal of Southern Africa...) Unique, to be sure!!

U _____ R _____ INN _____THUH _____ SHO!!!

Evolution?? Don't even tell the dragonfly — HE IS A DINOSAUR! His body is large, yet sleek, and his wings (structured like nothing else seen since the days of the WWI bi-planes and their wing-walkers) do carry him aloft. What does he care? He knows other dinosaurs could fly, and as the hovering-hummingbird-like creature he is, laughs as we try to predict his darting ability, and enjoys his flight. So it is with Fletcher's Faculty – some of whom think they have no talent – Avast Ye Lubbers!! Ye must and WILL participate in this year's Follies Show! Look who has already signed up!!:

- Kommander Kandace Celly: In her constant efforts to teach her JNROTC cadets how to find true north, will use her tallest, skinniest recruit, completely cover him/her with lodestone, slam him onto the first passing reefer (don't get excited – that simply means refrigerated) truck driving 84 MPH, and heading towards Central Canada!...(Nice plug for Igloo Hearts, Inc., Kommander!)

- Jair Skansik: Not sure his class fully understands life before abolition, will re-enact some typically antebellum tasks....on his property...taking 17 stupid kids, whipping and forcing them ('How Dey Wish Dey Wuz In Da Land Ob Cot'n') to clean out his attic, basement, and garage, re-roof and paint his house, and, using his pet dachshund as a mule, have them plough and plant the back 40 acres, all the while he is being fed grapes and fanned with ostrich feathers, (or is that fed ostrich and fanned with grape leaves?) His way of showing them that democracy never worked very well anyway, I guess. Who else? Skansik Legree!!

- And, Brother Hal Wyldir will create a mural...wellll, more like a velvet painting of Elvis, on our auditorium stage curtain by using a mixture of two parts tempera paint, five parts olive oil (all available at his retirement store – 'Starvin-Artists-R-Us') and threatening his class with indelible tattoos of a naked likeness of Andy Warhol on their earlobes, having them use only a double-ended Q-Tip, to produce an authentic Faculty Reaction to Fletcher's Year-End Testing Program!! – If you've never seen insanity personified, you don't want to miss this one, folks!

Don't even start with me! Tell me NOWW!

Bill, I plan to:

Seeeeeng _____ Impersonate uh (an): _____
Monologgg_____ Contact Lens _____
Woofer _____ Jugggl_____
Albatross_____ Key Lime Pie_____
Confetti_____ OR _____
YORR NAIM _____

PUBLIC ADDRESS, AKA - THE SQUAWK BOX...

So, as if I hadn't already bombarded them enough with the countless paper flyers to promote an interest in The Follies, I continued the barrage with messages tossed at them on the daily afternoon announcements. This second line of attack was to get on the P.A. system, disrupt all the classes, and annoy the students. Yes, the last 5-6 minutes of the day were always awaited with great anticipation, anxiety, and...FEAR! It's no wonder that so many speakers were ripped out of the wall.

Yes, Fletcher...it's true! Several teachers are offering incentives and special rewards when you come to the Faculty Follies Show and show them the program the next day:

Mr. Groceberg will let you wash his car for FREE! You Go, Teach! B.I.Ology will give you your choice of dissecting a specimen: An Amoeba? Or A Formaldehyde Frog!? WOW!

And Dr. Shure will reduce a late paper penalty from 50% to 46%! Is she a trooper or What??!

This has been, is now, and will be forever! AMEN!!

• •

And, just why are Faculty Follies such a smash hit? And, why is it considered the Spring Fling Thing to do? What's the reason you cannot afford to miss this Fletcher Laff-A-Thon?? Because it's brought to you by NHS!... (which the teachers have finally figured out stands for Numbskulls, Hollow-Heads, and Salt-For-Brains!!* (*And now, even the membership of NHS has finally figured out what those three letters stand for...Nerds Hoping for Sainthood!)

Follies! Thirty-seven teachers doing some very un-teacherly things! —

• •

Well, this just in from Law Professor Laing...We now have access to the private telephone number for Congress. Write it down...1-800-JUGHEAD!

Word has it that the Follies Show will feature the Social Studies Department posing semi-nude on stage...OH, Stop That! You don't REALLY believe that Skansik, Kooper, and Roddin are going to wear speedo thongs, do you?? Puh-leeze!!

Finally, don't forget that rotaneS elpruP spelled sideways is Purple Senator!

This has been a Sheela The Wonder Platypus Enterprise Production, Y'all!

Follies!! Brought to you by the stuffy staff we call teachers at good ole Duncan U.!

Wait'll you see your teachers in action...PLEASE wait! We need all the time we can get!

This has been one of those slo-mo things, Y'all!

• •

OKAY Fletcher — picture this: Departments of Foreign Language, and Language Arts ALL in Bikinis!! Got it? What? NO! NOT MR. SILBUS! What's wrong with you!? Good Grief! But, you never can tell what some teachers will do on stage...

This has been a Spring Fever Enterprises Production From NHS.

• •

NOW, you don't REALLY want to miss out on these great groups tonight:

Jimmy & The Juggernauts; Zorba & The Zookeepers; PLUS Sarah & The Sizzlin' Six!

SOOO, OK, Boys & Girls...The long-awaited field trip to Fletcher Senior High School is on for tonight! I checked with Mom and Dad, and they said YES...You CAN stay out till 9:00 and bring everybody home for a slumber party. We will have fun, cookies and milk, and re-live the raucous behavior of your almost teachers from Faculty Follies...Now all you need to do is shake down some poor unsuspecting freshman for $3.00 so you can buy a ticket. Jacksonville Beach Police will be cruising and will arrest any teen-ager NOT in the auditorium by 7PM! Who loves ya, Bubba? You got that right!

FOLLIES, YEAH!...

• •

Things You Can Buy For Three Bucks:

* Almost half a flick ticket — (what a good idea THAT is!)
* A few Krystal Burgers — (if you don't pay the tax)
* A box of chalk — Gosh! For REAL??
* And shoe laces for baby brother — unless he's into Velcro.

Follies, Man — That's the ticket!

...Now, I'm not saying that I'm proud of having been awarded the "Thug-Of-The-Year "trophy for 17 years running, but, I truly would have done ALMOST anything for my beloved Faculty Follies Show to be presented each year.

Most likely, I had more fun with it than anybody else. Over the decades, the faculty and staff of DUFHS have traditionally been some of the warmest and funniest people on planet earth. Their patience and willingness to put up with me on an annual basis is worthy of a mammoth trophy in itself.

HEY, TEACH! My heartfelt gratitude to you. GO SENATORS!!!

• •

[By their own admissions, many of the great comics (especially stand-up comedians) got their start in show business by doing impressions and/or impersonations. If that is true, than imitation is at least a high form of flattery. Not in an injurious or mocking manner, mind you, but genuine admiration: "That is really funny!" "How cool is that?!" "I wish I could do that!" or, "I wish I'd thought of that first!"

This next group of flyers was, in all probability, my attempt to compete with David Letterman's 'Top Ten' list. Well, obviously, my efforts were never any serious threat to Dave. Be that as it may, they did manage to capture the attention of several teachers and staff members, as I succeeded in corralling them into participation in Fletcher's Fabulous Faculty Follies.]

• •

TESTIMONIALS: FAMOUS CREATURES FOR FLETCHER FACULTY FOLLIES

1. Lady Liberty – 'Give me your poor, your tired, your huddled-masses, your ragged, your talentless, star-struck, etc…And her buddy, Br'er Rabbit – 'Zippity Doo Dah!'

2. Milli Pede – 'Hey Teach, wanna dance? I know a thousand-steps!' And her good friend, Miss Piggy – 'I go hog-wild over the Follies!'

3. Yosemite Sam -- 'Faculty Follies! Ya Dig?!'

4. Tony The Tiger – 'Follies? They're Gr-r-reat!!'

5. Olive & Oscar Octopus – 'We were walkin' down the beach, hand in hand, in hand, in hand, (uh, sorry), heard about the-Follies & broke out into a round applause, and a round of applause, and a rou….' (OK! I'll stop!…)'

6. Dahli Lama – 'Life is likened unto that of a beaver – One Dam Thing After Another….' (What's that got to do with The Follies?? Dam if I know).

7. Tooth Fairy – 'The Follies have deeeeep roots!'

8. Jack Frost – 'Follies: That's coooool!'

9. Jiminy Cricket – 'PARTICIPATE!…Or you will feel guilty for the next eight minutes! (And always let your conscience be your guide)…'

10. And our Fine Feathered Friend, Foghorn Leghorn – 'The Follies, Son, Ah say, The Follies are really a fun, I mean a fun activity, Boy. – You understand me, Boy? Golly, pay attention, Son!'

Gee Bill – U R SOOOOO Persuasive! Put me down for any 17 acts, but my BIGGEST talent will be….

Thanks Folks, Barnacle Bill

Now, just in case you think Faculty Follies is of no consequence, check out these Ten Spinoff Shows Given Birth By Da Follies:

1. Who Wants To Be A Dullionaire?? (…and yes, this question is worth $100.00).

2. Just Shoot Me…(Don't Tempt Me!) since re-named Law & Disorder Starring Tom & Tammy Teach-A-Lot & The Mindless Muffins.

3. King of Queens & Bishops & Knights & Rooks & Pawns (formerly entitled Fluff Daddy & the Talentless Twelve), & soon to be re-titled A Legend In Our Own Minds.

4. Kathy Jung & The Restless & The Mutants & The Soon To Be Imprisoned. (Possible name change to Mayhem at P.S. 223).

5. The Bold & The Beautiful & Those Not So Kindly Treated Or Well-Endowed By Mother Nature.

6. The Axe Files: Herman & Harriet Hatchet Face, & Tom A. Hawk, Producers – (Previously known as Frolicking With Fletcher's Fab Five).

7. Wheel of Misfortune (which superseded the ill-fated Buffoons Of The Vampire Slayer).

8. Touched By (your choice):
   Ann Gelieri
   De Angelice
   An Arab…
   (careful…I do not take kindly to irreverence!).

9. Attack Of The Teen-Aged Turnips!!

10. HEY TEACH! DON'T GIVE UP YOUR DAY JOB, AND EAT LOTS OF RIBOFLAVIN!! (an obvious attempt to placate Byl Munck who felt slighted that I left off everyone's all time favorite family classic, Leave It To Cleavage…)

Gosh Bill!!! You win again! I can hardly wait to be in the show and be:
   A Mutant
   A Frolicker
   A (WUTT)??
   A Rrested

TOP TEN REASONS TO PARTICIPATE IN THE FACULTY FOLLIES:

10. All your life you wondered what it would be like to be hit in the face with a large, juicy, over-ripe tomato...

9. Stephen Spielberg needs a star for his new flick – "Jurassic Punk".

8. You are such a role model for our youth as they see what 4-8 years of college can accomplish...(hmm).

7. FIRST PRIZE: Two weeks (9 days, 5 nights), NO expense paid trip to Mayport where you just might get to talk to a REAL sailor! Let's hear it for May, MAY, MAYPORT!!

6. AFT/NEA/FEA/DTU are all looking for new lobbyists who can sing & dance.

5. Minimum wage for all participants will increase to $3.08/HR at midnight sharp, June 33rd.

4. In exchange for our participation, our illustrious School Board has promised that we can teach their new perform ing arts curriculum, and they ALWAYS keep their promise, (don't they?) right? RIGHT!

3. Miraculously (& mercifully) talent scouts are all deaf and blind one night a year.

2. My Uncle (Andrew Lloyd Webber (Weber?)) needs a cast for his new Broadway Production about a mysterious talk show host. It's called "Phantom Of The Oprah"...(just hush and read # 1!)

1. 'Afore ah joynd thuh Phakultee Pholleez, ah kud nott spel TEECHIR, 'n' noww ah R won (Juan), one, wun?

(...Sometimes it just seems right to use the words Faculty & Folly in the same sentence...)
You make me smile, — Grazi, Teach — William

SOME FAMOUS FOLKS COMMENT OF FLETCHER FACULTY FOLLIES:

1. BILL CLINTON: Fletcher Faculty Follies are even gooder'n eatin' a Big MaC (or three)…Yummy! Wow!

2. JANET RENO: Everybody has a constitutional right to be stupid.

3. JIMMY-THE-GREEK: 8 to 5, they fold after one night.

4. SAND L. WOOD: (Izzatt about surfin'??…)

5. MIKE TYSON: Oh No! It's too embarrassing, soo, I'll just whisper in your ear………...

6. TOM COUGHLIN: All right! We're gonna have 3-a-days in full pads till April, or until yuz get it right!

7. (A) H. Y. ENA: Ha! Ha! Ha!
    (B) S. CLAUS: Ho! Ho! Ho!
    (C) J. MICHAEL MOUSE: Gosh! It's enough to make your head spin and make ya Dizzney!

8. FLORENZ ZIEGFELD: F O L L I E S , MA N ! That's The Ticket!!

9. UNITED STATES DEPARTMENT OF EDUCATION: (Jeez, Abdelnour – will you just give it a rest??!)

10. JERRY SPRINGER: Could use just a tad more sex, cussing, and violence. (Enter the Math Department).

Okay, Bill, OKAY, O-K-A-Y!! You win again — I promise I will do the following in The Follies Show:

Yew R Alll God's Children & Luvvd by Billy Boy

FRED AND FLORA FOLLY!
ALL OF THE FOLLOWING EXCUSES FOR FOLLIES PARTICIPATION HAVE ALREADY BEEN USED UP:

1. The Hale Bopp Comet cometh again!...I MUST PREPARE!!

2. I was on my way to your mail box WITH my Follies form in hand, Bill, and , NO JOKE, I was attacked by this paper-eating dog, and, well – you know...

3. I never perform for less than 13,000 (people &/or dollars).

4. I've been meaning to, Bill, but I've just been so busy counting my Congressional Medals of Honor and all like that...

5. WHO YOU CALLIN' A FOOLY, FELLA?!

6. I promise, Bill — as soon as I establish world peace, conquer-global hunger, and figure out my income tax – you can count on me for Follies!

7. BILL! The darndest thing happened! While I was fishing and pondering my Follies performance, a cop came by and arrested me! (Of course, there WAS a sign there that said NO FISHING ALLOWED, but Bill – I promise — I was being REALLY quiet...would I lie to you?...)

8. Not unless I get points or hours credit toward my certificate, or 20% gratuity (whichever is higher).

9. My Follies form was sitting right there on my desk, and lo and behold (I've always wanted to lo and behold something), lo and behold, I knocked over a burning candle, and, well Fahrenheit 451 and all like that...

10. It is against the tenets of my religious denomination – (WG5 — We Got Good Go Get-'em Gospel)...we're not permitted (or aloud) to perform during any April which has a Tuesday in it...

Just Tayk My Wiird, Sahib, -- YT YZ PHUNN!!
Bill Abdel(The Friendly Arab)nour

GOOD THINGS THAT JUST MIGHT HAPPEN WHEN YOU PARTICIPATE IN FLETCHER'S FABULOUS, (YET POSSIBLY FAULTY), FACULTY FOLLIES, FABLES, FOIBLES, TOMATO, TOMAHTO...

1. You win the lottery...and you didn't even buy a ticket!

2. You stop getting students who have the mentality of quinine.

3. Your neighbor's pit bull develops a terminal case of periodontal disease (or PYORRHEA, if you're over 39...)

4. IRS discovers an error in your tax return and refunds you a check for $14,812.07...Yeah – ranks right up there with your purchase of ocean-front property in Utah.

5. On your survival course in Indonesia, Komodo Dragon is on-your menu and does NOT 'taste just like chicken'!...(I know: 'How is that a GOOD thing?'— just leave me alone — I'm a nice guy!)

6. O.J. is convicted of something, by someone, sometime, somehow, somewhere, for some reason.

7. 'Inventions R Us' wants to market your new gadget – a lefthanded tomato seed extractor...(WHAT'D HE SAY??...)

8. You don't get in the bank teller line behind the person who's building/buying three condos, two strip malls, and exchanging 113,628 yet-to-be counted pennies for paper money.

9. A 12-pound bag of M&M's will not add 12 pounds and 12 inches to your waistline by the time you finish the bag in 12 minutes...

10. You're voted Teacher-Of-The-Hour, Day, Week, Month, Year, Decade, Century, AND Millennium all because you gave some kid a BIG B-I-G-G smile by participating in Fletcher's Faculty Follies Show — You Go, Teach!!!

Big Bill "Bully" Abdelnour and NHS
(...and don't forget — AYE GNOW WAIR U LYVV!...)

Chapter 16

Talent

...The-Proof-Is-In-The Puddingly speaking, we now take a look at some of these 'Gee Whiz, Bill – I don't have any talent' types who balked 'n' walked 'n' talked 'n' squawked a mile-a-minute trying to get OUT of the show...time that could have and should have been well spent on preparing some little tidbit for the annual 'Sillies of Springtime' caper known as The Fletcher Faculty Follies. Absolutely unbelievable what they came up with to share with colleagues, students, and, indeed, the entire Beaches Community –Song 'n' Dance, Skit 'n' Mime – such imagination buried deep down in their modest souls.

Much of what they produced surprised most of us – including themselves! How much fun it is to laugh, and even more so, to laugh at one's self. Check out some of these acts invented (or stolen) by our illustrious faculty. Embellished? You Bet! Fun and Funny? You Bet! Duncan U. Fletcher? Flunkem U. Betcha!!

• •

[So as not to run out of ways to embarrass my colleagues, of course, I embellished their introductions at show time. Indeed, as master of ceremonies of the Fabulous Fletcher Faculty Follies, I took the full wide range of license, leeway, and latitude at the microphone. (Also helps explain why I was selected as the 'GERITOL-FOR LUNCH-BUNCH' Poster Child, and earned the coveted SENIOR-CITIZEN-RUN-FAST-AS-HELL-TO-ESCAPE-THE-WRATH-OF-THE-IRATE-TEACHERS AWARD, as my Olympic track skills became better and better each spring at Follies Show Time...if you know what I mean...)]

• •

Still in demand at used car dealership openings, The Upper Michigan Sugar Beet Festival, the Ribbon-Cutting Ceremony for the Super Wal-Mart in Downtown Greater Buzzard Gizzard, Arkansas, and the Dust Bowl Park Rally to Save the Sandspur – for your listening pleasure, because they finally made it From Boys II Men! (In a minute, you'll see why these guys know nothing about haircuts, but know a great deal about Barbershop Singing!) Ladies & Gentlemen, please welcomeTHE SOCIAL STUDS!!

INVISIBALL: When I was a kid, one of my favorite magic tricks was watching the man catch the invisible ball. After many years of practice, I have also mastered this trick. Since it is invisible, you won't be able to see it, but listen carefully, and you will be able to HEAR me catch the ball in this paper bag, and a round of applause on each catch will be greatly appreciated. Ms. Phalin, toss me the ball, please…And for my final catch, I will catch the ball in my pocket and show it to the audience…just in case you had any doubts…

• •

'Ein Stalag ist ein prison, numero zwei hundert drei und zwanzig!!'…and if I mispronounced any of that, PLEASE don't tell Mr. Dolloway…he is ALSO one of my former students…(Where did I go wrong??) An Obvious Escapee from Freddy's Funny Farm, you will enjoy a Misery-Loves-Company performance by Han Dolloway!!

• •

KARNAKOPIA I: Ladies & Gentlemen! He's back! The Middle Eastern Marvel (Muddler) Rides again!! The Mysterious Mystical Fourth Wise Man who came to the manger!! The Sage who knows the answers to questions before they are even asked! These answers have been concealed in a bubble gum machine and buried behind the deserted Pic'N'Save store on Beach Boulevard. (OR)…Have been vacuum packed and zip-lock bagged in the teachers' coffee machine) since 6:22 this evening…(OR since, oh, about 8 minutes ago). Folks, here to amaze you, please welcome warmly and tolerantly, The One, The Only, KARNAK-THE-ALMOST!!!)

KARNAKOPIA II: Once again, the mysterious sage from…well, parts unknown, really,…has graced us with his presence, to demonstrate his uncanny ability to know the answers to questions, before he even KNOWS the questions! These questions have been thermodynamically sealed in an abandoned conch shell buried behind the Drivers' Ed. Range since 4:17 this afternoon. An Honorable welcome for KARNAK-THE- IMPOSSIBLE!

KARNAKOPIA III: Just back from an almost successful 5-day/2-night stand in Pascagoula, Mississippi – this Mysterious Man of the Middle East has the unique gift of prophecy to know the answers to questions BEFORE THE QUESTIONS ARE EVEN ASKED!! These questions have been ice-brewed, freeze-dried, sealed and concealed deep in the soap dispenser machine at the local laudromat since sundown, and he has no knowledge of their content! Please welcome, – KARNAK-THE-MEDIOCRE!!!

• •

You may know Salt & Pepper, You may know Sugar & Spice – But you ain't seen nothin' yet, - This next foursome is NICE!! Put your hands together for SWR – SISTERS WITH RHYTHM!!

• •

The last time these folks sang, the entire audience was converted...TO ATHEISM!! NO! NO! NO!...Their husbands were turned into salt??...Well, you know – these ladies can really sing! Ladies and Gentlemen, give it up for Klawdy Marshyl & Francy Parkkir,

The Good Gospel Gals!!

• •

Last year the impact of the Human Bowling Ball was so strong, it rattled the trays at the Tastee-Freez all the way down in Palatka! While teaching at Perry Tarker, Tomm LaMoynt lost all of his marbles...Believe me, he has LOST ALL OF HIS MARBLES!! Just watch Tomm as King Pin as he goes for his 67th. straight perfect game!!

• •

Rajah Woody has more friends than you can count! Among them he includes Tarzan of the Apes, Shamu the Whale, and the NBC Peacock! Applause for the Class Menagerie!!

• •

If you heard it through the grapevine, you heard it right, 'cause here is the fruit of that shriveled up vine. Please welcome the Hoot

of Hoots! Stitch of Stitches! What can I say?? Here they are — (…
and please remember, patience is a virtue…) Harmmonn, Moover, &
Wawkee!! – WHITE BREAD RHYTHM!

• •

Tem and Jehn thought a long time for this act: Original names considered were The Blow-Up Twins, Dyna & Mite, TNT, Nitro & Glyc-
erine, Fire & Works, Pyro & Technic. Folks the cell phones under
each of your seats are connected directly to the Fire Department and
911!! Here they are — The Prince & Princess of Pyrotechnics! The
Conflagration Kids! Give it up for Terrible Tem and Juggernaut Jehn,
— EXPLODO!!

• •

Tonight I will try to fulfill a life-long dream of mine -- conducting
the New York Philharmonic Orchestra playing the William Tell Over-
ture. See ya' in about two shakes…better make that 92 shakes!…
(looong pause)…Wellll, as soon as this old man catches his breath,
we will continue. Was I good, or what? Do you think The Lone
Ranger will forgive me?? My Dear Heart keeps trying to tell me that
I'm not 21 anymore and now you see why (puff, puff, puff); anyway
it will always remain ALLL dream.

• •

Remember your kindergarten teacher? Well, you just wish you had
one like this. With a vocabulary all five-year olds are learning, her
method of teaching the alphabet is unique to be sure. Please welcome the Shady Lady, - Ms. Mandi Shaydee!!

• •

A harmonic, symphonic group of four voices (Makes one wonder
how did they EVER con such a group to sing in combo?? Bomb-o be
more like it!) Ladies and Gentlemen, The Voices Ride Again! Please
welcome back The Social Studs!!!

• •

So, You think Aretha got soul?! Man, don't even TRY me! We got
Aretha, Samantha, and Davette! You don't EVEN know what I'm talk-

ing 'bout...They've gained RESPECT; They've gained their FREE-DOM; AND She's Still The One & Only, Suze "Aretha" Harrmonn!! AND, if it's Homerun or Triple - It's time for the RIPPLE! Fudge Ripple! Just do what I tell ya! Here they are – The Queens Of Soul!!!

[MORE P.A. JAW AND CHIT-CHAT]

(The following is a "Could the $58,000 your parents spent on your college education been spent on something more productive??" presentation, y'all!).

Hey!...Now listen! — Did you ever stop to think of the fact that Speed Limit spelled backwards is timiL deepS?? NO?? Gosh, some of you really know how to waste time, for goodness sake!! Well, one thing you better do is save $3.00 for — And ponder this:

Follies, Man —
Faculty Follies — I'm talkin'
Fletcher Faculty Follies!!
34 teachers and some of them can READ!

This has been a Dollars for Scholars Presentation — You Got that Right!!

• •

Well, there used to be a dance it was called the Macarena,
Everybody did it because they were insane-uh,
But teachers could not do it, because they have no brain-uh----
NO! NO! NO! Macarena!!
(This has been a : 'Can my teacher really walk and chew gum at the same time without tripping over his own shadow' Presentation, Y'all.)
3 bux; 34 teachers!

• •

The following is an 'I'd Walk A Million Miles For One Of Your Smiles' Presentation, Bubba: Hey Listen! We have singers, dancers, musicians – Shucks – two of them can even carry a tune (yeah, right – in a bucket, maybe!!!)

Hey Fletcher – Escuchen! When you go to Follies, there are some teacher rewards for you:

For Example: #1 Ms. Shay will give away autographed copies of her new (sure to be a best seller) book, 'Half Noisy Off The Eastern Back'…AND NO, it is NOT a cheap knock-off of that other WWI novel — 'All Quiet On The Western front'!! #2 Mr. Woody will let you dissect some NEW specimens. NO, NOT those scrawny little cats, frogs, & earthworms...But, how about a 17 foot giraffe,…or even a…what's that? A mastodon??? Yer cool, Mr. Woody!! And for those who like formaldehyde, he'll even save the containers for you!! NOW, is he a trooper, or what!!?

This has been, -- don't you agree???? I thought you would!!

• •

OK! Now those of you who have finally saved 14 hours pay to buy a ticket to Faculty Follies, please be advised that there are possible side effects; such as:

1. Waking up at 2:30 in the morning with uncontrollable laughter; OR,

2. Forgetting to feed the cat, dog, or goldfish for 3 days after the show. OR,

3. The urge to hug your teacher the next day and say, 'Hey, Teach, do that crazy thing you did in Follies, AGAIN!' OR,

4. A loss of toes and growth of third ear, or second nose!; OR,

5. Best of all; You will not be busted for loitering on the Board Walk and saying – 'Hey Sailor-Boy, — Wanna have a good time??' (WHAT'DHESAY!!)

This has been brought to you by the 'That Was The Best Three Bucks I Ever Spent In My Life!!' Corporation, Bubba and Bubbette!! U R LUVVD !!

• •

OK – Time to call on the powers that be: HEAR US O SPIRITS OF THE COAST!!

- Great Kahuna of the salt, We truly all beseech —

- Briny caretaker of all, our inner souls please reach —

- And Sol, you epidermis tanner of those that look like bleach!!

- Yes, you armadillo hunter, and surfer on the beach —

- Help me make it to the show put on by those who teach!!

- (Don't Even Try Me!! Just Do It!!)

- This has been a Matter-of-Gray-Matter, Y'all!!!

• •

So Yeah — We got your basic Two Thumbs Up teachers in Da Follies:

Have you not seen, Lean and Green Mean Machine – Myk Laveen!!
We got yer basic Tia Toni Phalin AND Science Royalty Tem Alyn!!
And nothing could be 'Wilder' than Brother Hal on his uke –
He plays it on a music box they used to call the Juke!

Just come to the NHS…Numbskull Hilarity Sensation!!

…Who Said That??…Big Deal! Lollipops & Roses!!

This has been an "Obviously I did not qualify for a part in 'Oklahoma'" presentation folks.

• •

…and speaking of Oklahoma, several great guest appearances are on tap for the Follies:
1. The ever popular, Jimmy & The Jugheads
2. Everybody's favorite, Freddy & The Flip Flops
3. The Current Rage, Sammy & The Sandspurs
4. And Special of Specials, a return command performance by Ree Groorml as his lead role in Oklahoma – Yes, 'Curly' will be singing his hit song in Kechni, Tagalog, and Swahili until he finally realizes that the "Bright Golden Haze On The Meadow" is NOT

gold at all and he's not gonna get one thin dime from NHS for doing this gig! NANNU - NANNUU!!

• •

Quick! Use the word cantaloupe in a sentence!: "We must get married in the church because we cantaloupe!"...Gosh! Where is a "Northeaster" proofreader when you need one?! So, if you want to be IN on the 5th., spend 3 on the 4th!!

FOLLIES!! N H S !!

• •

Say Gang...Do your teachers have talent, or what?...What'r you crazy??? Of COURSE they don't have any talent! Why do you think they're teachers? Gee Whiz!! But Sister Slue-Sugarfoot Suze Harrmmon will give 17 free tardies to all students who come to the Follies show!

• •

And Brother Hal Wyldir, using only a cup, a pencil and a rubber band will create more music than you could ever get from an orchid!...HMMM... This has been and will be again, Y'all!!...Yes, Folks—all in all we have 40 YES FORTY Fabulous Fletcher Faculty in our show...and coincidentally, 40 is exactly the age of each teacher in the show...(Well, either that or the average IQ of all of them combined...Flip a coin on that one.)

This has been A Two Hours Of Good Times
Guaranteed Presentation, Fletcher.

• •

YES! It's true! Halin Furness DID promise that she will treat all who attend Faculty Follies to a gourmet dinner of Filet Mignon, escargot, caviar & a 37-yr. Old bottle of Chardonnay wine that'll surely tickle your taste buds and palate! So, you can see it is really...Aw, shucks...wait a minute. I had it wrong. Really sorry. That gourmet dinner will be only for those who make a 7 on the A.P. Exam. Follies attendees will be taught how to say and spell Krystal Burger...She is alllll heart!!

Today is Thursday, You know what that means – We're gonna have a Fol-lies Show!!! AND by the way – still wondering what you cannot buy for three bucks? A few reminders:

— A Maserati and A Corvette – both cost more than $3.00

— Open Heart Surgery costs more than $3.00

— Your favorite pizza? Topped with watermelon and paint? Can't touch that for $3.00.

— And offering a bribe to Patty Shay or Jetty Lolly for a passing mark in English – DEFINIITELY costs more than $3.00!!

BE THERE: $3.00!!

• •

What? Stop that!! Beaufort! Down! Down Boy!! Dern dog about swallowed the microphone —

Somebody feed that mutt please!! OK,... Folly-filled faculty, 7PM... Doors open 8PM...UH, 6pm...(hmmmm, maybe it should be 8...) a dollar for adults, but only a DOLLAR for children... Good Golly, Molly...we'll be looking for you, and BEAUFORT says "ruf"... Which is hound dog for Be There!!

• •

Good Mornin' Fletcher High School!!

Tomorrow, Tomorrow! You'll love us tomorrow...We're only a day away!! Some rewards from your teachers if you come to the Follies:

• Julna Tommis will show you how to crack the ever tough equation, $2X=10$...

• Tem Alyn??, Well, Tem will show you how to practice the always profitable Reverse Oxidation by turning real GOLD back into cast iron... Seems he wants to give credit for that one to his buddy, Al Chemy (...Yeah — I give up, too.)

- And, Jay Deckit will demonstrate the power of transfer by substituting the screech of his trumpet to that of a garden hose & funnel.

So, c'mon — $3.00, 60 nickels, 3 GW's, 30 dimes...we'll take it all...But we WON'T take American Express!! (OH, Baby, you KNOW what I like!)

Follies! $3.00! NO GREEN STAMPS! GOOD GRIEF!

• •

(THE LOVABLE LESTER AND VERNON AS PLAYED BY THE EQUALLY LOVABLE COMIC, JIM VARNEY)

Hey, Vern! What's that? You want to know if our principal is any kin to Victoria Principal??... Dern you,Vern! You really make me burn! When ya gonna learn? Ya know what, Vern??? Yer kinda on the low side of dumbernhell...

Hi, Vern! Yer right — Follies Tonight! Really? You wrote a letter to the newspaper about Follies?! That's great, Vern! Tell me about the letter...It was a "W"...

I see...No, that's okay, Vern. My fault. I did ask... thinking all the while you had more sense than God gave a thumb tack!

Vernon, Vernon, always late...When you gonna graduate?\

You been here since '74...They're gonna push you out the door!!

Vern, just how many Folly shows have you seen??....All of 'em — yeah, I kinda figured you did — I hear you were almost in one... what happened?... Didn't qualify as a filly — No, Golly Vern — It's not Filly, it's FOLLY!! You know what Vern? Fletcher ought to get a diploma when YOU graduate!

Thirty-eight teachers performing the unbelievable...REALLY UNBELIEVABLE!!

(And, yet, more micro-babble…..)

If I could talk to the animals…Well, Rahja Woody can and does. Believe me when you see this act, you'll know why he's building an ark and expecting 40 days of rain….Everybody! Rahja Woody is Brother Noah!!! (OR)….How much wood would a woodchuck chuck if a woodchuck could chuck wood???… I don't know, but Rahja Woody does!! Big Round of applause for a gift to the Animal Planet… Mr. Rahja Woody!!

• •

This next pair has managed to elude all efforts to capture them and be placed in an insane asylum. When you see this act, you'll know why most people don't want to mess with them!! The Two! The Only! Tomm LeMoynt and Myk Laveen!!!

• •

This man is obviously not afraid of losing his job. He says what, when, and how he feels! Yes, folks, he is still at large! Still ranting and raving and still shouting educational injustice… Here he is - a round of applause for Dangerous Han Dolloway!!

• •

The volatile ingredients for this next act were flown in by Galactic Express from Hong Kong, Beijing, and the Planet Krypton!… well, actually, these two guys ARE from Krypton!!… Anyway… here they are… X and Plode, Tem Alyn and Rahjah Woody, (one of my former students)… Gosh! For Real??!

• •

The Patience of Job, The Wisdom of Solomon, The Voices of Angels… Wellll, your teachers don't have any of those, BUT they do give a valiant effort to singing some songs they have worked really hard on. Please welcome your Fabulous Fletcher Faculty Chorus!!

• •

Maybe ACTING silly, and being SILLY are not the same thing (and stop looking at me as if I qualify for the latter!), but damn if it isn't fun watching nearly 200 years of college educated teachers trying to distinguish between the two. Did we miss our calling? All bets are off. Were we the products of a mis-spent youth? All bets are on.

If we did not have a good time, then sharks don't have teeth... (hmmm – don't believe a word my colleagues tell you...) The Amateur Hour lives, folks. Talent? – it's only a word. Shakespeare, Mozart, Terpsichore, The Mormon Tabernacle Choir would have loved us. So there!

• •

We Were Gonna Sing Barber Shop Quartet But We Couldn't Find Seven Guys

• •

...Now, I'm not saying that arm-twisting and intimidation are the best or only ways to win friends and influence people, but I did win friends and influence people... (welllll, maybe not as many as I did make enemies...) Upon my retirement, I'm told that my efforts at Faculty Follies stands as somewhat of a legacy and institution at Duncan U. Fletcher Senior High School.

I hope my esteemed colleagues have – at least first and foremost – forgiven me, and had as good a time with it as I did. (Incidentally, – if you are thoroughly convinced that you 'Saw It On The Oprah Show', chances are pretty good that it was not about our Senior High School Production).

Chapter 17

Colleagues

...Pedagogically speaking, teachers are indeed a rare breed. Species, perhaps qualifies as an alternate choice of terms. Most of us always resented some stuffy evaluation given by an administrator who had not been in the classroom in 5, 7, 8, 10 years. They know all the jargon, terminology, and catch phrases which helped them earn their Ph.D., Ed.D., or M.Ed., but had no earthly idea of how to actually teach or handle the kid (in an overcrowded classroom of 37-42) who could not read, write, or count; and – consequently, had the personality of a wounded rattlesnake!

Departmentally, a group of 10-20 teachers becomes a rather tight fraternity/sorority. We care and cover for each other. We share in our family joys and sorrows. When one of us retires, the remaining dozen have lumps in our throats, the size of golf balls. It is rightfully a passionate and emotional time. Here's to all the pedagogues!

• •

[Five good teachers all left Fletcher High School at approximately the same time. Each time I was asked to come up with a few friendly barbs and kind memories on their behalf. Never one to turn down a chance to get up in front of an audience, here are some of my personal thoughts and feelings for these folks as they left the teaching profession, and some of the fun we had teasing these five teachers upon their retirement. In honor of: Barnhorst, Wirdn, Allbirt, Harrs, and Stynkrau.]

• •

WIRDN/BARNHORST

What is it with Senior Class Sponsors?? As long as I've been here, ALLL of them have been from the Social Studies Department (OK.... one exception – Lotijin was one of those science types – jeeez!) Barnhorst, Passeenger, Abdelnour, Durlee, Furness, Sakirdot...Do we have a monopoly on stupidity?

At one time, Evon Wirdn wanted to be a Senior Class Sponsor. Up till then, it was just a natural that Barnhorst, Abdelnour, & Durlee were the sponsors. After all, the Senior Class was very much aware that our initials spelled out BAD! If Wirdn came in,...BWAD or DWAB…just did not convey the same message of fear to the seniors. Just wasn't the same as BAD! Sounded more like Elmer Fudd!! Somehow, I just can't imagine Michael singing and dancing to "I'm BWAD! I'm BWAD"!

Lately, Evon has sent me some of the kids she had in her earlier honors classes. At first, she sent some really nice, bright, fun-to-teach kids…THEN she cancels all that out by sending me Kevin, Brian, and Mark…Now, maybe these guys were not all losers, but they DID already have prison numbers on their shirts when they walked into my classroom!

One time I saw this kid…(KID…looked like a cross between The Incredible Hulk and BIGFOOT!). Well, anyway, he popped off to Evon at the wrong time…

A particularly BAD HAIR DAY for Evon, as I recall…Without breaking stride, she picked him up by the armpits, and hung him on the "EXIT" sign above the door at the end of B-Hall! Promise! True Story! She won the Christmas Door Decorating Contest that year, which was interesting, since it happened in April…

There always seemed to be a shortage of women in the social studies department, but the ones we got – MAN, they were good!!… (okay, WOMAN, they were good!!). Easy, Evon! Don't hit me with a Title Nine – Chapter Fourteen PLEEEEZE!!

Our resident Flaming Liberal is not only a great teacher, but let me tell you how she handles discipline: Evon could take care of a wise guy with a simple SIT DOWN! SHUT UP! OR, 'What's the matter? You take a wrong turn this morning?? The Junior High's across the street!!'

Waylon and I both taught Evon's children. Equally, bright, challenging, witty, and personable as Mom. We will truly miss you, Evon.

• •

Groundhog Day, 1973, – a particularly rainy February 2nd., – the scuppers on the gymnasium roof had been originally constructed too high to drain properly. Tons of water had built up and were now sitting on the gym roof. Leaks had been reported for days, weeks, months about an impending disaster. Our illustrious school board, of course, chose to do nothing about it. 2:40 p.m. Basketball team had just finished a light practice, when the T-Beams lost their camber, and the roof came crashing down. On my way back from bus duty, I see Purl Wyte coming quickly from the girls dressing room: "Hey, Purl, what's happening?" And just as calm as the sunrise, she says: "The Roof Is Caving In..." I said, 'SAY WHAT'??

She repeated, "The Roof..." I earned an Olympic gold medal running out of that building...So did Waylon,...So did Purl,...So did everybody. It sounded and felt like an earthquake, and ten minutes later, after viewing the damage, and oohing, and aahing, Waylon & I were BACK IN THAT BUILDING...doing what? Moving cases of paper for the ditto and mimeograph machines...I said, "Waylon, what's wrong with this picture?" He said "WHAT"? I said, "We're standing ankle-deep in water saving paper in a building which might collapse on us any second...He said, "RIGHT...So what's your point?? Let's stack it on the tables so it won't get wet..."AND, like two dummies, WE DID!!

Now, Brother Barnhorst (Department Chairman) kind of defies description. Is there ANYbody here who has NOT received some "Free Fatherly Advice" from Waylon??...Solicited or otherwise???

And how about some of those doozey schedules and assignments he handed out in years past? (1) Okay, now Jair , you and Haylin will have 9 preps each...SEMESTER. (2) Roice, you and Max will alternate between Dumpster Watch and Smoke Alley Patrol. And (3), Evon, let's get that textbook order in – we're not due to have new books for another twelve years!

Waylon was always able to finance your expensive wish list purchases by concealing them somewhere in the 2250 account. Remember that? Everything from 12 cubic feet of the Great Pyramid, to 14 cattle prods, to one Lear Jet, to three live members of the French Foreign Legion!! How'd you do that?? Chairman Laing, pay attention! EMPIRE BUILDER – BARNHORST ENTERPRISES!!

One day, Waylon just happened to mention to me that there was a big shirt sale at May-Cohens. I said thanks, Bub – I really do need some new clothes. So, he went by and bought a half dozen; next

day, I went by and bought a half dozen; and the NEXT DAY…
We met each other in our team-taught classroom, and we FROZE!!
MIRROR IMAGE! We looked like the same person with Mutt & Jeff
heights. We both wore our new shirts: Same brown & yellow striped
shirt. Same tie. Same pants, belt, shoes, socks!! All we needed was
a hat & cane! If we heard Bobbsie Twins once, we heard it 4800
times that day. Cornelius Ryan thought that 'The Longest Day' was
about the Normandy Invasion. Let me tell ya, folks – For Waylon
and Bill THAT was the longest day in the history of planet earth!

By the way, these two venerable warriors have prepared one last
act of concern for their fellow man, and that will be to open up a
new restaurant next month called Old Fogies 'R' Us! Yes! And their
specialty will feature an entrée combination of dinosaur and hog…
they're going to call it Jurassic Pork! Evon! Waylon! We love you both
and we're damn sure gonna miss ya! God bless and take care.

• •

AL ALLBIRT

Landmark Middle School asked me to MC the retirement of Al
Allbirt. Obviously, they did not know, but Fletcher HS does: Bill
Abdelnour in front of a microphone = DANGEROUS!, Sooo, what-
ever happens, blame Al's principal – She said I could do this.

Al Allbirt and I go back a looooong way. In the MAT program at
JU, Al gave a presentation on WWI. Al lined up all of his toy trucks,
tanks, and soldiers…It was as close as he could come to being
'Stormin' Norman Schwarzkopf'. He still looks like him a little bit,
don't ya think?

Al's had several jobs in 29 years in the Ed. Biz. Before Landmark,
he was with us at Fletcher for 15 years as teacher and curriculum
coordinator. Before Fletcher, ITV. Before ITV, Landon Senior, Junior, Middle school…Kind of makes you wonder what's left?... A
stint with the Avant-Garde-Pre-Natal-Center-For-Embryos?

Speaking of Landmark, what a great name and location for a
school. Landmark barely won over the second best name: Pow-
erline Middle School. I'm not saying that the magnetic field gener-

ated by the power lines is strong, but just before they corrected the problem, it had created a 16 car pile-up because of a mass of metal drawn to the school driveway consisting of three semi-trailers and a railroad car loaded with Sears bicycles. As a matter of fact, at night, Kernan Road glows in the dark and serves quite well as a runway for flying electric eels and UFO's. Both Al and Lou want us all to know for any questions or concerns, please feel free to call her back any time in her lead-lined office, on her new toll- free number, 1-800-VOLTAGE.

Al perpetrated a lot of craziness at Fletcher High. He was so impressed with his own title: Cur-ric-u-lum Co-or-di-na-tor, Assistant Principal In Charge Of Curriculum: All that just to be able to say: 'Yeah, kid – I know you're 22 years old, and yeah kid – you STILL have to pass English.'

Some think Al was too soft as an administrator, but let me tell you, I've seen him in action. A seasoned veteran teacher came in complaining to Al that she had to have this, that, and the other, and that she needed so-and-so and la-de-da. Al looked her straight in the eye, gave her 8 sections of P.E., and 7 sections of Algebra II... Boy was she sorry she ever opened her mouth – she was a home economics teacher!

Just a few years ago, Al had an Oldies Radio Show, called Doo-Wops & Bee-Bops. It came on at 10 AM Saturday mornings. Anybody remember that?... Gosh, look at all the hands...must have been a real smash hit, Al... Well, anyway, I was a guest DJ with Al on that show one time. First 12 minutes of the show, we were nearly arrested three times for being "less than professional" on the air. Al had assured me that we could use those seven words on the radio. Two Live Crew? Who R U?? Eat your heart out!! He continued that talent as DJ playing Beach Bop music at 57 Heaven every Thursday night. Good Show, really!

We have an annual teachers talent(less) show at Fletcher called Faculty Follies. One of the acts consisted of Al, myself, and a couple of other teachers of history, government, and economics. We called ourselves, -- what else? -- The Social Studs...everyone thought that was pretty cool...except for our humorless principal...

Al also did a pretty mean Dennis Miller in his Senior News Update, – he managed to alienate every twelfth grader in Fletcher.

But all these experiences pale when compared to Al's life-long passionate love and knowledge of pop music. Al has a collection of 87 million 45 RPM records. At one time it did number 91 million, but Al lost a few mistaking them for skinny Frisbees, or very thin licorice doughnuts, and as we all know, a doughnut's chance of surviving Al is similar to that of a snowball in Hell...NON-EXISTENT!

Al and I always play a musical trivia game; we ask each other who had the hit recording of ABC, or XYZ, and my record is perfect. I have never missed one...Well, anyway, here are a few of Al's favorites for which he probably thinks he knows who did the original, but he will probably be surprised to know the real artists:

Let's try these, Al: Rock Around the Clock — (Al) "Oh, too easy! Bill Haley & the Comets." Well, no, Al...that was actually done by Tommy & the Tick Tocks... Let's try another one... Lonely Teardrops — (Al) "Ah Yes! Mr. Excitement! Jackie Wilson!" Uhh,... wrong again, Al; that was done by Clara & the Cry-Babies,...Well, Al, – you seem to have hit a cold and dry spot here; I better just tell you the rest of these.

"How Could You Believe Me When I Said I Loved You, When You Know I've Been A Liar All My Life?" That, of course, was done by the Famous Freddy & the Filibustering Fibulators.

"I'll See You In The Spring, If I Can Get Through The Mattress"... that great hit, for sure, was done by Buffy & the Bedbug Bedmates.

And finally, "Antlers In The Treetops"...by Hoo Goost the Moose?! (...yeah, I know...kleptoed from the 1950's...so sue me!). So, what can we say about the Big Bopper, The White Man's Chubby Checker, the guy who taught all the great DJ's how to broadcast – Yes! The Grease Man, Alan Freed, Hoyle Dempsey, Dick Clark, Casey Kassem, Wolfman Jack, & Murray the K. — Al taught 'em all. And, some day Al, when you're up there in that great Disco in the Sky, you'll know that whatever the music, they'll be playing YOUR song!

We Love You, Al! May God Bless! Enjoy!

HARRS/STYNKRAU
(FACULTY LUNCHEON PROVIDED FOR FHS BY U.S. ARMY)

Yeah, Yeah! I know, I know!...'Oh Boy! Just what I need – another 20 minutes of jaw after a big meal'...(when all I really want is my pillow and blanket!).

And how 'bout that meal?! What a menu – amazing what they can do with the left-overs from the invasion of Panama!!

Aw, cool it, Sarge! I'm just joking. Besides, you can't draft me; I've done my time – Spanish-American War,... (the FIRST time we won Miami away from Cuba) – AND, YES, I have every confidence that we can do it again! BUT, I digress...

It's only fitting that we honor two such outstanding teachers as Marilu and Jym today. We did have a problem with what we should call this great gathering of eagles. A couple of suggestions we had were The Geriatric Version of the Ken & Barbie Show... OR, The Prune Juice For Lunch Bunch...take your pick.

And look who they ask to Host the Roast!!! To honor two giants in the highly skilled and technical disciplines of MATHEMATICS and SCIENCE...Right,...a second generation Syrian who can spell calculus and physics!!...and just so you'll know, YES – there are TWO Z's in fizzixx!...

But not to worry about their replacements. Dr. Pawk's been right on top of that situation and has already narrowed the application list down to a Final Four of sorts. Last week he just finished the last of his interviews with that foursome: three armadillos and a fork. Reliable sources say to put your money on the fork...BUT, I digress. MARILU HARRS – the mere mention of her name conjures up a picture of the Scourge of A-Hall! T'is true! Students would rather swallow a bowl of logarithms than enter her classroom! She makes good on her threat to bend any kid into an isosceles triangle if he DARE to show up without homework in hand; with God knows who (Tom Selleck, Paul Newman, or Hulk Hogan) playing the part of the hypoteneuse!

Marilu started teaching under contract when a teacher's salary was a whopping $2700/yr...every year...for ten years...and that was back in the year 19...yeah, that's right...the year 19!...Must have been a fun decade.

Marilu has been around a loooong time. She's been to Grad Nite with the Senior Class so many times, Walt Disney World wants her to be a permanent fixture on Space Mountain! So, now they'll have Mickey, Minnie, and Marilu Mouse.

How does she do it at her age?? We know for sure she taught Euclid and Pythagoras, and rumor has it that she even taught Larry Pawk at Andrew Jackson High School — in the 50's — THE 1850's!! Now, when she gets up here she's going to tell you that she even taught Bill Abdelnour at AJHS to which you are to respond LIAR! LIAR! But for her longevity and endurance; her ability to survive the rigors (or rigor mortis) of teaching; her resilience and stamina in persevering the strains of the profession; and for making it a better profession because of her continuance, we thank her and we WILL miss her!!

Now, JYM STYNKRAU started teaching back when teachers PAID THE SCHOOL BOARD for that privilege, and we ALLLL know how fond of the School Board Jymbo is: "SAY WHAT?? TAKE A HIKE MACK!!" Actually, Jim never called them Mack. His favorite names for them were Jerks Unlimited! BUT, Ya know, except for a few cases of bad luck as a youngster, Stynkrau could easily have been President of IBM, Chief Executive Officer of Dow Chemical, or yes, even the inventor of NINTENDO (whose original name was really JYMTENDO anyway). But the innocence of youth took its toll on Jim. E.G.:

1. He botched up his chance with NASA because he never could spell $E=MC^2$.

2. His classmates never got used to him saying 'Please pass the sodium chloride' at lunch.

3. He missed 2/3 of his 7:30 classes in college – obviously practicing the law of inertia: a body at rest remains at rest until moved by an outside force, oooorrr, simply put, LET SLEEPING DOGS LIE!

4. And, his buddies never could convince him on Friday nights,

that when they mentioned going out to get some leg, breast, and thigh, they WERE NOT talking about Kentucky Fried Chicken!

But a trooper he is. Any day now, he expects to receive a patent for his latest endeavor: Yes, that remarkable, multi-purpose, two-in-one substance, Doc Stynkrau's TOOTH PASTE & WALL ADHESIVE! SON OF FLUBBER?? YOU BET!! Golly, Sir Isaac Newton would be SOOO proud of him!

For Marilu and Jym, retirement is only a word. They both intend to stay active in their fields of expertise by offering their services as consultants to those in need. They will call their new company RENT-A-FOSSIL...

Thanks Jym for all you did for the kids and the concern you had for the teachers' union in your many years of the teaching profession. You are truly a trooper.

Marilu and Jym, we wish you Godspeed.

• •

...Now, I'm not saying that every single teacher is or was worth his salt, but the Morton (When It Rains, It Pours) Company could stay in business a looong time if it checked out all the NaCl in the fields of education. Down the road, we all might meet in that great faculty meeting (or faculty lounge) in the sky. Should we take the roll? Make a seating chart? Collect the homework? In any case, let's not forget our re-admits and hall passes. 'Ms. La-Dee-Da, can I go to the...?' And for goodness sake, don't forget the combination number to your locker! Schooool, Teechir!!

Chapter 18

Retirement

...Efflorescently speaking, they made it! The Flowering! The Blooming! The Peak! The Fulfillment! The Crowning Victory! THE TEACHERS' RETIREMENT! My college pal, Rudley said it best: 'That great gettin' up mornin' finally dawns. The day you wake up and realize for the first time that you are retired. How sweet that must be. Like all the first days of summer vacation rolled up into one.' Yes, I know — look out LPGA, Olympics, Mt. Everest, Trump, Turner, Gates! Runaway Best Seller! Here I come! Soooo, what can I say, Teach, except – May God Bless, & GO FOR IT!

• •

RETIREMENT PARTY FOR ABDELNOUR & GYRR
(SOCIAL STUDIES DEPARTMENT)

(Departmentally, we roasted each other with friendly barbs galore. What a blast!)

With bittersweetness, Jymm and I both appreciate this VERY nice sendoff and farewell party. But, I have made some observations about this department over the years, and I want to share them with you.

- My next door neighbor and sharer of room noises, Ryk Benk is about to become a new papa. That's great, Ryk! We just want to make sure you know the proper response to give for whatever your wife says for the next few weeks: Ryk, Honey, – will you get me some artichokes and truffles, please?: [Wrong answer: But, sweetheart, it's 2:30 in the morning!!] [Right answer: Yes, Dear]...So, just get your butt up and go get the artichokes and truffles! Good luck, Pal! Your life will never be the same!!

- Rob Rodann: Florida History! RAH! Rob was so excited first quarter – some kid took only seven weeks to learn that Florida is a peninsula, and Tallahassee is the state capital! Way to go, Rob! Rob had some rather unsavory kids on his basketball team and is still working on getting paid for mileage on his car for his countless trips from Fletcher, to home, to jail, to home, to Fletcher, to Juvy Hall, to home, to jail, to Fletcher, to

Juvy Hall to jail…and STILL hopin' to see one of his players make it to the NBA without becoming a new papa, convicted felon, member of Mike Tyson Fan Club, or drug addict! We're pullin' for you, Rob-O!

- Mal Broley: Mr. Security! Kids cut him a wide path when they see him coming! Ever see him walk the halls? Oh Yeah! Bull Whip in one hand, Cattle Prod in the other! 'Ya'll stop that kissin' now! Button your blouse! Get up off the floor! I'm not gonna tell ya again!'…I think we all agree that we'd rather see one Mal in the halls than five campus cops!!

- Jay Chelker – One of the bright new faces in the Social Studies Department. She's also a Fletcher grad, along with Krissy Bonner, for whom Waylon and I were Senior Class Sponsors back in the '80's. This year Jay took on the unenviable and thankless task of putting together a departmental World History quarterly and final exam…Soooo…She and Krissy jumped right on it like good little doobee eager beavers; – Max and I, of course, looked at them like they were from another planet…

- Krissy Bonner: Thoroughly convinced she had taught too many Fred and Flora Freshmen, too many Sam and Suzy Sophomores…You know the ones – they're always too cool to learn about The Constitution, Congress, Democrats/Republicans; too cool for Caesar, Charlemagne, Elizabeth, Napoleon, or Churchill. Krissy still wonders why God even made some of those little teen-age urchins…

- Otto von Bismarck, Rush Limbaugh, General Patton, Jerry Clower, and MAX KOOPER!!…Need I say more??…Ever see Max get in some kid's face??! Man, I mean a work of art to rival Picasso, DaVinci, or Norman Rockwell: 'What do you MEAN you did not know??!! Yes you DID know!! Now give me that sub-machine gun before I make you eat it!!' You are one in a million, Max, – and stay that way, Bubba – Those are the best odds I can give you!!

- Tee-What-A-Good-Sport-Bribok! He's been in EVERY Faculty Follies Show since 1980…and sometimes he's had good reason NOT to be, and he'd make his case to me: 'Bill, my house

burned down and my family is being held captive in Siberia!!'
Of course, I listened and responded compassionately, 'Gee,
Tee...I'm sorry to hear that, but that's okay...you're not in the
show until acts 5, 7, & 10!!...

- The skillful, wonderful Haylin Furness! 10,000 things she has
done WITH me and FOR me, and NEVER complain...(well,
ALMOST never). Senior Class Sponsor, Classroom Teacher
Extraordinaire, NHS Sponsor, Shared Decision Making Committee, Faculty Follies, Chaperone, Grad Nite, AP Coordinator, and ALL with such Furness finesse. It's no wonder. She
has earned so many Teacher-Of-The-Year Awards, she has
wallpapered her entire living room with those certificates!!
And, oh, yeah – she is still the only lady I know who can
pronounce her beloved city in South Carolina in one syllable
– CHOLLZtn, and everybody STILL knows what she's talking
about!! Haylin – Yew R Thuh Besst!

- Jymm Gyrr is just plain happy to be getting out of this crazy
profession. He is, however, making one final contribution to
Duval County. He told me he is very close to developing a
new breed and specie of flower designed just for the School
Board – I think he's calling it The Bloomin' Idiot?!.. Is that
right, Jymm??

- There are still a few of us left in the Social Studies Deptartment that
some folks call Blue Collar Teachers – Jair Skansik is one of them –
well, even though he wears a white collar every single day!!
Jair can shave, shower, and get dressed in exactly 8½ minutes!! Dee Dee has his tie and lunch ready as he walks out the
door: Bye, Dear! See ya later! (And don't you love the way
he responds to the malcontents? – Hey, Mr. Skansik – How
come you gave me an "F"?? Skansik, in his ever inimitable
way: 'Because they wouldn't let me brand your forehead with
an "I" for IDIOT!!')...Stay meat and potatoes, Jair! We need
guys like you at Fletcher!

- EDD Laing: Mr. Chairman! Mr. Chairman! Still tries to accom-
modate all departmental needs and requests, and STILL hoping someday we can distinguish between those two: EDD –

can we get some glow-in-the-dark pencils?? EDD – how about some SCANTRON sheets with 800 bubbles?? EDD – I NEED my own copy machine AND 12,000 reams of paper!! But, y'all be careful now. If he continues to be as efficient as he is, JEB, or George, Jr. will probably draft him to be on the Supreme Court. Can you imagine…? We'll actually have a justice who can read, write, and count!!

- Steev Ortee – What a guy! He handles the annual $50,000 project of the Junior/Senior Prom, copes with some uppity rich kid who wants to bring his date to prom in a helicopter, and STILL prefers teaching 9th. graders!! What is wrong with this picture??! Preferring to teach freshmen, is like choosing vanilla ice cream over rocky road! Get over it, Ortee! Nobody likes 9th graders!

- Well, maybe Byl Munck is not all tied up with technology, BUT – did you notice the last bulletin he put out? Must have been a Freudian Slip because instead of Byl Munck, he signed it Bill Gates???!!! Inadvertent, unintentional, Freudian Slip? Like Hell!! If that's not deliberate, then God didn't make little green apples, and Foster's NOT Austrylian for beer!! Think about it: He ponders the world of computers and assumes, 'Well, doesn't everybody have an office that looks like the cockpit of a jet airplane??' He walks in, his eyes roll back into his head,: 'Hard drive to Modem – This is Techno-Sparks One – Come in Modem, Over.' Cranks that Screen-Saver up to Crunch…And of course, from Techno-Maniac, to the three Klutz-Techno-Phobes in our department…Yes, it is true – if he gave Kooper, Skansik, & Abdelnour one letter each, we probably could spell IBM! We still don't know Lap-Top from Lap Dance! Oh, by the way Byl…Amie said the next time you come home lit up like an electrode, you WILL sleep in the carport!…Oh, you already do?? I won't touch that one…

I know I speak for Jymm Gyrr as well as for myself when I say thank you soooo much for this warm, outstand-ing, sendoff party. Take good care old friends, and buddies, and all my friends from Social Studies.

· ·

MY FINAL FACULTY MEETING
...ON MY RETIREMENT

I am a slob...I will cry...SO WHAT?? You know I'll not go down without a fight.

I've been picking on you people for years...Hell, some of you, DECADES!!

Currently, this faculty has at least 11 teachers for whom I was either their teacher, or Senior Class Sponsor, or NHS Sponsor or all three, much to their consternation! Over my tenure of decades, I'm sure there were probably at least a dozen more who have come and gone through the mighty doors of Fletcher Senior High School... What on earth possessed you folks to become teachers?? I thought I taught you better than that!

· ·

I do have just a bit of concern for our beloved JJ girls – Jozee & Judy – Let's keep an eye on what will happen to their stock in the Hershey's Chocolate Candy Corporation...After all, not many of us are able to walk into their office, load up all four pockets with candy, put seven pieces in our mouth, and act like we're conducting business, and Lo & Behold (as one who was able to accomplish that feat repeatedly and always looking forward to Lo-ing & Beholding), Lo & Behold – THE BASKET AND BOWL ARE NEVER EMPTY! A Sweet Tooth from The Sweetest gals on staff!!

· ·

I've been here for all of the principals Fletcher has ever had. From Roggett, who hired me, right on up through Ellie Monn...and friends, we have had some beauts, haven't we? Now Ellie knows she is exempt from this next little barb, but at times it was embarrassing when people would ask us who is the principal at Fletcher, we had to reply, 'Well, we don't have a principal, we have da-da-ra...'

· ·

I always wanted to host a dinner for one Charles Lee Skot. You know – a very long dais with many friends and colleagues all taking friendly verbal shots at him…Just think, it would be a genuine Chuck Roast!!

• •

The only reason some of you are unhappy that I'm leaving is because now you have to move your mailbox up, down, or over one! Oh yeah – and that alphabetical teacher board in the main office?… Here we go – Angeleero, Allin, Betty Brown, Kovey Browne, Campbell, Cantrell, Cartir, Donovan…

Some of the Grading Bubble Sheet comments need to be altered or replaced. How about some of these instead?:

- Dear Dad, marry this girl off early! Give her a thousand bucks, and send her to Folkston, Georgia NOW!

- Dear Mom, someday your son will make a good doorstop or paperweight!

- Dear Parent, sell this kid for eight cents/pound while the market is UP!!

- Dear God, why did you waste the $2.80 worth of chemicals making this kid's body?!

- Stop naming your kids Kalisha, Bundorkiss, Shalondra, Quiniella, Rapunzel, Marquista, LaTisha, Malisha, Hay-zus, Rampelstiltskin, Sheldrika, the III! Those are not names, those are sounds! Give your kid a chance! Let's get back to John and Mary!!

Karnak have a few more predictions:

- Ellie Monn will tell you, "Well, it's just one more thing you have to do," sixteen times before the first progress report goes home.

- Karl Dansen will still be here when these walls are little more than the remaining ruins of what was once a proud, great, and mighty high school…

- And, in the year 2040, Pat Shay will STILL BE A HOTTY!! Is she a BABE or what??! AND, does Eddie Shay know that I'm madly in love with you???!

Ellie has already told me that it will take another good Seminole to replace me...or...14 Gators!!...And by the way Fletcher, y'all keep that Seminole/Gator/Bulldog/Hurricane thing going...that's really fun!!

The next time a foul-mouthed kid gets 'In Yo Face, With A Big Disgrace'...'Not me Sucker,...You MUST mean someone else!'!...Just back off,...count to eleven,...Think about ole Bill...And then – HIT HIM JUST AS HARD AS YOU CAN!!!...I PROMISE, I'll come visit you in JAIL!!

Next time I see you and offer my perennial greeting: 'All I want to know is just how in the Hell are you,...and I want to know right NOW?!... You BETTER have the right answer.

Take care of my school, Fletcher...It's still the best high school in all of North Florida...AND don't let ANYBODY tell you different.

I hope you miss me...I'm damn sure going to miss you. Thanks for EVERYTHING, and may God Bless you.

• •

...Now, I'm not saying that teaching is the do all and end all of all professions, BUT, it is way the Hell up there on the pecking order. If people have not spent a few years in the classroom, maybe they ought not be so damned critical of those of us who have.

Time and learning are history. As soon as you say 'now', it becomes 'then'. You are not now the same person you were when you began reading this book. You are a few hours older...and you can just feel the gray hair sprouting from the top of your head as we speak!

The world's great historical figures have quite often been the world's great teachers: Aristotle, Moses, Jesus, Charlemagne, Elizabeth I, Martin Luther King, Jr. If we have not learned from the past, we are truly condemned to repeat it...(where have I heard that before???) Long Live The Teaching Profession!

• •

Chapter 19

Luncheons

...Retirementally speaking, it is so nice to be remembered, and especially, remembered fondly. I finally left the teaching profession in 2002. One year later, my colleagues, once again, asked me to be the MC for the retirement dinner honoring eight more of my friends who all left Fletcher at the same time in 2003. I was thrilled and honored to be so highly regarded – especially since I was not even on the faculty anymore.

• •

FLETCHER RETIREES LUNCHEON, 2003 (FRIENDLY ROAST)

Having had a year's head start on them, I had several useful bits of information for the retirees. It just doesn't get any better than this!

Hi Everybody!! I must start off by simply saying, – I AM TOTALLY INTIMIDATED!! You see, some of these people are so old they were MY teachers. Combined, they have been at Fletcher over 180 years! So, bear with me, please...I will calm down in a minute.

We would especially like to thank all the cows and chickens who gave their lives for this auspicious occasion. Their 'MOOS & CLUCKS' did not go in vain. The Chef told me that in the interest of preserving the retirees, some of whom are ancient, a bit of caution was used in placing just a tad of preservative in their drinking water hoping they would last through the entire luncheon; so a little sodium propionate was given to each; you know, – just as a precaution to retard spoilage...

I'm having a bit of a problem with this word RETIRE. Yes, some of you know that already. In transportation, it's easy. To RE-TIRE means it's time to put some new wheels on your vehicle. They're worn out, – the treads are gone – soooo – RE-TIRE. OK,-- but in education TIRE means to witness FATIGUE...You're not exhausted enough already?? You really want to try it AGAIN???!!!! – What is wrong with you??!!

At this juncture, I was going to try to put you in a good mood by having a little rhythmic audience participation by teaching you the Mighty Sewanee Hand Clap. Legend has it that this tradition was born at the University of the South, Sewanee, Tennessee...(We're not sure why, other than the theologians in seminary have little else to do up there on that cold winter mountain sometimes...I guess you can only meditate for so long). Well, my mind was quickly changed when Zelle, Jozee, and Frann all reminded me, with uncanny accuracy, that White Folks Aint Got No RHYTHM!!

• •

Sometimes I think those who make it to retirement genuinely have 'The Right Stuff' to start their own reality TV show...SURVIVOR: JAX BEACH!!

Just look at this group of purists. They want to do something different than have TV Land make the Beaches Red Cross Station look like some ominous ruins. Nope, -- they want to go to the original source; the undiscovered continent of Plato; the continent of ATLANTIS!! I don't know what the big deal is – at their age the only continents they have to worry about is INCONTINENCE!

Can you imagine the endorsements and testimonials they'll be offered in the near future? Gosh, contracts will be coming out of the woodwork!! Sign right here to plug the following: Depends, Dentu-Creme, Support Hose, Pepto-Bismol, Poli-Grip, Botox, Zippers, Velcro, and Viagra!! And, when they do go on those nice trips to those fancy hotels, instead of a chocolate mint on their bed pillows, they will now find a piece of foil-wrapped Ex-Lax!!...AND, Y'all have to stop worrying about the expiration date on all products. ESPECIALLY, buttermilk, yogurt, sourdough bread, and sour cream! The operative word is, after all, SOUR! And, unless there is a layer of bluish/green mold on top, you sure as HELL can't tell by sniffing it! Get on with it! LIVE LIFE!

[What's that? Karnak is here? WOW! The Mystic Sage From The Middle East!: ...Billy Graham, Loch Ness Monster, Glutton-For-Punishment: ——

*Name a Preacher, a Creature, and a TEACHER!!]

Don't ya just hate it when you hear that ALL great educational innovations started in California? Good Grief, to hear them tell it, California invented air, salt, sand, sea, and surf! Berkeley, Santa Barbara, San Diego State, Southern Cal, San Fran, UCLA. And how avant-garde the language they use to invent and label a new course. With a double dose of Educationese and Jargon so thick you can cut it with a knife, they sound something like this, sooo raise your hand if you ever had to take a course with the following titles:

Philosophical Foundations of Education

Foundations of Educational Philosophy

Educational Philosophical Foundations...yeah,...that's what I thought. Therefore, translation: 'We have absolutely no idea what we're talking about!'

Next time they start on you with that nonsense, you would do well to just remind them all of what the abbreviation for California, the first five letters of that state, C A L I F ——— REALLY stands for: Come And Live In Florida!! And by the way, when they start telling you how much better California citrus is than Florida's, there's only one way to tell...

Punch a hole in the orange, suck on the juice, and if it sucks back...IT IS ABSOLUTELY A CALIFORNIA ORANGE!! You positively have my permission to tell them to Go Directly To Hell!! DO NOT Pass Go Or Collect $200.00!!

And how about that Cracker Jack State Legislature we have? It took them longer to decide on whether or not to extend the DROP Retirement Program than it did for the glaciers of the Great Ice Age to melt!! The Hundred Years War took less time! Golly Molly! They should all be sent back to their planet of Erklefitzzenquizzel, or some place!

And, speaking of The Ice Age, ever wonder how old Coli Jimson is??? No one seems to know. All we know is that it's in the three-digit range, and rumor has it that C.J. has gone to having a birthday every OTHER year! Good move, Coli!

Over the decades, I taught many of the same kids Coli taught in English. They'd often come back and tell me how peculiar it was trying to take notes in Mr. Jimson's class. It seems Coli never leaves ANYTHING to chance, and so he dictates every single item he wants them to know. Witness his lecture on the Great Northern Epic Poem, BEOWULF: Now (comma) the Great Giant (comma) Beowulf (capital B) (comma) basked in the reputation of his mother (comma) Grendl (capital G) (period). (New sentence). Grendl (capital G) (comma) as we all know (comma) had a grip like the Incredible Hulk (capital I, capital H) (exclamation point!) (New paragraph)!... Am I saying that must have been a king-sized drag? Well, four kids had to be treated for head injuries because they fell asleep in his class and their heads hit the desk! AND, the only reason I know that is because the same four kids fell asleep in MY CLASS!!

Any of you folks remember when Coli had an Afro hair-style? Sam Jaffe – pay attention. Honest to goodness, back in the '70's; it was so curly and puffy... I'm not sure if it was by choice, or if he stuck his finger in a light socket! All I know is that he made the perfect White Man's Jimmy Hendryx! Really cooool, C.J.!!

I have a limerick for Brother Jimson. Hope the meter is right... otherwise he's over here with his red pencil giving me a C-.

Of Shakespeare & Beowulf & Grammar,
On these topics ole Jimson did hammer –
'Twas a thrill & a half,
His class got the last laugh,
He's entered the Retirement Slammer!

And NO! We did not know that ANGASAL spelled sideways is LASAGNA! And YES! We can conjugate the verb to DISCOMBOB-ULATE!!

You're one Helluva guy, Coli, and an absolute legend at Fletcher High School.

Bon Voyage, Friend

• •

Still hoping to have some kids read 25 books this year? Shair Shurr has hopes that some of her kids can SPEAK or WRITE 25 WORDS without stumbling! And for goodness sake, let's make sure they know that not EVERY sentence starts with 'LIKE!!'

'Like, Mary, he has a body, like to die for! Like I nearly fainted when he like said hello to me at my locker! Like he's the bomb, like!!' TRANSLATION:

SHE CRAVES HIS FLESH!!

Dr. Shurr wrote her Dissertation on Sensitivity to Students' Needs, and she really does have the patience of Job with MOST of her charges, but sometimes even SHE loses it. I remember one time a kid came back to her after report cards went home, and asked: Gee Whiz, Dr. Shurr, how come you gave me an "F" for Failure!?" Shair glared at him and said: "Because I can't give you an "L" for Loser or an "N" for Numbskill!! Your mother dresses you funny and you have the mentality of CHALK!!" She never cracked a smile...that kid cracked, however,...into 17 pieces!

One of Shair's classes was a real Doozy! They were supposed to write a paper on an original topic. Well, you could almost predict what they wrote. Gosh, the names on her roll book for that class were none other than the likes of Ricki Lake, Jenny Jones, Maury Povich, Judge Judy, Jerry Springer, and Montel Williams. Topics?? You guessed it — "I was a Teen Aged Light Bulb," "My Mother Married a Cactus", and "People Who Eat Rubber"...Needless to say, Shair demoted all of them to the seventh grade.

Shair has big plans for retirement. She's going to start a new enterprise to supplement her income. All Senior Citizens will be able to economize and stretch that fixed income dollar by patronizing her new innovative dual company – Sherry's Vitamin Vault & Car Wash. But wait – that's not all!! — For $9.95, you also receive an 8"X10" glossy of Shair posing with a real live bus driver. AND, for $3.00, she will even autograph it for you!! What a Gal!!

You are a strange lady, Shair, and we hope you stay that way.

• •

Max Kooper is going to retire, kick back, and, of course, write The Great American Novel...What am I saying??? Max Kooper IS The Great American Novel!! (Or Novelty!) What a character.

One of Max's all-time favorite personalities was an old southern humorist named Jerry Clower. Clower was one of those good ole boys who was very proud of his Dixie heritage, and not prone to take advice from those beyond the Mason-Dixon Line. One of his favorite expressions was one Max holds dear to his heart: It simply goes – WE DON'T REALLY CARE HOW Y'ALL DO IT UP THERE IN CLEVELAND!!... And you know Kooper...he always overdoes everything: Therefore, anybody north of Mayport is a DAMN YANKEE!... And, any place west of Macclenny is a foreign country!! TRANSLATION: Shut-up and pass the butter!! I mean what else would you expect from a guy whose two favorite pizza toppings are broken glass and concrete!!??

One day Max's classes were giving oral reports on various good topics. Sooo, I paused for a little while, and sure enough, some interesting things were going on. Kids were talking about Napoleon, the Russian Revolution, Egyptian Pyramids, the Great Depression, and WWII. The next kid gets up and starts expounding to us about one Ira Q...Milt and I looked at each other...neither one of us had a clue. Twenty minutes later, Milt figured it out...The kid was reporting on the country of IRAQ!!

You know, folks, Max Kooper has often been Coach Kooper for many good teams here at Fletcher: baseball, tennis, football, golf. I played golf with Kooper one time, and this is a true story. Now, you gotta understand that I put the DUFF in the word DUFFER. Well, on the first tee, I got lucky and drove the ball about 180-200 yards right down the middle of the fairway. Max says, 'Nice shot, Bill'. I said, 'Thanks, Max.' Okay, so Max tees up a brand new ball, takes a whack at it, and SWOOSH!...Out of bounds, hits the road, lands in an 18-wheeler semi-truck passing by,...winds up in Palatka...probably the longest drive Max ever hit...So, he says: 'I think I'll take a Mulligan'. I said okay. So he tees up another brand new ball, takes a swing and BANG!...slices it off into the woods never to be seen again. He said: 'Bill, let me try again'. I said sure. Sooo, he tees up another brand new ball, swings and POW!... hooks it left and splashes it into the middle of the lake... He's about to tee up another brand new ball for a fourth try, when I said, 'Max, if you have that much trouble hitting the ball straight, why don't you use an old golf ball??' He said, 'I NEVER HAD ONE!!'

When his darling wife finally puts him in a home, he'll still be coaching. The games, however, will be a little different: shuffleboard, monopoly, basket-weaving, bocci, curling, and croquet. Thinking about starting his own TV game show called "Bowling for Brussels Sprouts". But, don't mess with Max. Last kid who whined, 'But I never WAS good in geography', Max gave him a one-way ticket to Afghanistan!

(And, by the way, Max — Jozee STILL needs your grade bubble sheets — FROM SECOND QUARTER, 1997!)

Max Kooper, you are one in a million...well, better make that TWO million!, and still the best arm-chair quarterback anyone has ever known!! Stay Kool, Kooper!!

• •

A few years back, my duty station was in the library with Norzell. Ever work with Norzell?? Only lady I know who could do eight things at one time! I'd walk in and she'd start: 'Mornin' Bill: - Newspaper's over there, these reference books need to be re-shelved, catalogue the rest of these books, magazines go back on the periodical rack, inventory is due at 11:00, file these glossy cards, if the phone rings, take a message, I have to take this purchase order to the principal and bookkeeper's office, be back in a minute... She had the only teacher's desk in the whole school with no chair, because SHE NEVER SAT DOWN!!

'Twas equally true of her predecessor, Frankees. A kid walks in, demands she finds what he needs, and Frankees is already swamped. Politely, she says: 'Young man, I'm really busy right now; see if you can get started by using the Dewey Decimal System, and I'll be with you shortly.' RUDE KID SAYS: Don't know no Dewey; Can't do no decimal; Ain't got no kind of system...sooo, Madame Librarian, just find it for me...my book report is due third period!!! And that would happen if they were looking for Dr. Seuss or a book on quantum physics. Gosh, talk about the patience of Job! I'd have been in jail a LLOONNGG time ago for hitting that kid! And poor Norzell, she got caught up and stuck with the officialese, and is STILL waiting for somebody, ANYBODY, to call it a Media Center, instead of what we've called it for decades, a LIBRARY!

But, ever genteel, Norzell and Frankees are donating three new books to Fletcher's library: 'Doorknobs of Denmark' 'Raising Earwigs for Fun and Profit', and their personal favorite, sure to be a best-seller, 'Thirty-Seven Things To Do With Belly-Button Lint' (not to be confused with the Blue-Lite Special at K-Mart, -- One Pint Jar — Thirty-Nine Cents).

You are a gracious lady, Norzell, and Fletcher will remember you with love.

• •

Remember the 'Peanuts' cartoon by Schultz? One of the Charlie Brown characters always had the answers to life at the booth which read: Psychiatry – 5 Cents? Well, Nann and Barbie had a similar sign at their office doors which read: Guidance – All you can handle for FREE!! Turling & Bonn; Bonn & Turling; Sounds like a law firm, for goodness sake! Ever see them lose their cool?? Never!... Well, ALMOST never… There were times when I'd rather wrestle a crocodile under a barbed wire fence than face one of them about student or parent so & so. Now folks, let me tell you – that's really saying something coming from this Ole Seminole…seeing as they are two of the most vocal Gators on planet earth! Seems their job descriptions never mentioned that Guidance required as much effort for 150 teachers, as well as 2000 students! Yet, sometimes, even those two Queens of Patience Galore could lose it. They'd walk down the hall in tandem, fishnet hose, stiletto heels, monocle and riding crop, and you knew you were in trouble: "Mary! You're getting a new student with A.D.H.D." And, of course, you'd say, 'Oh No'… Then they'd continue: "But THIS time, YES! IT DOES stand for Another Damned Hopeless Dolt!! Sooo, you really were justified in responding to the kid,'Attention Deficit My Foot!! Pay A-Damn-Tention!!'

Not sure you know this, but one time they were on some Best Friends game show. Wheel of Questions, or some such biggie.

The couple ahead of them were asked to name the first three letters of the alphabet. They missed it! Nann and Barbie rubbed their hands and could hardly wait to answer. Moderator says, 'OK, ladies, your question: Name seven left-handed Lithuanian surgeons... I hate when that happens!!...

The Guidance Gals are going to open their own bookstore/ reading room/café for retired teachers...you know, something like Barnes & Noble. But uh...prerequisite to that happening will be for them to read the book called 'How Not To burn Kool-Aid'. Menu will be a bit different. Instead of Danish, biscotti, and latte, they'll offer oatmeal, granola, bran and fiber muffins, Geritol and prune juice!!...MMMMM...They haven't decided yet whether to call it Fogies 'n' Fossils, or Geezers 'n' Geeks...Good choice, ladies! Just let us know when the Grand Opening is scheduled...

• •

Pat Shay: My, My. How many countless times has she been in charge of ALLLL the Hearts & Flowers occasions; ALLLL Faculty Parties; ALLLL Retirement Recognitions; ALLLL Secret Santas & Gift Exchanges; ALLLL the headaches of Prom along with Steev Ortee for the last ten years or so; AANNDD, willingly served on the Faculty Follies with Jady, Maree, Mandi, and ME year after year. You'd think she would learn! That show is always IFFY at best, and more than once, we totally BOMBED! Folks, I'm talkin' Atomic/Cobalt/ Hydrogen BOMB! I remember now and then she did take time to ponder: 'Now, let me get this straight: You want me to bust my brain to come up with an original act to perform before 300-400 kids, make a total spectacle of myself, and all for some ungrateful NHS snobs to get some college scholarship money???????? Sure sounds like something I want to do!!

And, some of you who have served on the NHS Scholarship Committee know what she means. My favorite application goes something like this: Yes, my folks do make $174,000/yr, but I REALLY need to go to (pick one) Dartmouth, Stanford, Duke, Vandy, or MIT, and tuition there is $83,000...A WEEK!!...Well, get over it kid. That's why students holler 'Go Ospreys, Go Seminoles, Go Gators' — because they can afford state education!! Either that or see if you can get into Mabel's Professional Body-Piercing, Modeling and/or Tattoo Parlor Academy!!

Like many elderly people, Pat has found religion. She plans to start a new non-denominational church called the 'We Got Good Gospel, Read The Bible of Solid Scripture, Apostolic, Pentecostal, Go Get 'Em Jesus, Holiness Temple'...

SAAYY YAAAYUS!! Patricia, we will all be there every Sunday, PROMISE!!

You folks all know the reputation Pat has of always being sweet, patient, accommodating, understanding, and compassionate... Wellll, I walked by her room one time and heard some kid belly-achin' about something...You know the whiner-type 'But, I didn't KNOW about the da-da-ra...and Pat, in a perfect Jay Leno response, gave him...Shut-up!! Yes you did! Stop cryin' about it and turn in the damned assignment!!!

Patricia has always handled aging very well. After all, she WAS born at a very tender age, and was only two on her second birth-day...(what'dhesay??)

Her next project will be especially for the retirees: She will host the First Annual Special Olympics for Septuagenarians...Of course, Pat will never admit to being 70 years old, so when that birthday arrives, we will all be celebrating the 31st. anniversary of her 39th. birthday!! Great idea, Pat! We just wish we'd thought of it first!!

I gotta tell ya, Faculty Follies was one of the loves of my life. But, BUUTT — They truly would never have happened without Pat, Jady, Maree, Mandi, and all of you crazies who participated annu-ally. And, the only one who laughed harder at Raja Woody and his Zoo Parade of Animals than I did was Pat Shay. AND, if I ask him to do his impression of the Gentle, Gigantic, Jungle, Jumbo, Jumping Frog of New Guinea one more time, he's going to jump right down my throat!! Raja, where are you, Bubba? God love you, friend. He was the inspiration for Mark Twain's tale of 'The Celebrated Jumping Frog of Calaveres County', and if you've not read that, you owe it to yourself to read a very funny story.

● ●

Jimmy Dowirtee has been around Fletcher in one form or another since 1911, and it might be just rumor, but I'm told he has gone to shaving in the dark...AHH, the ravages of age...

At one point, Jimmy pulled up stakes and moved to Okeechobee. NO, I DO NOT KNOW WHY...But, curious and pushy that I am, I asked him. 'JIMMY, Why on earth did you move to Okeechobee??' He said, 'Well, Bill, I always wanted to see the sugar cane grow.' Gosh, next to watching paint dry, I can't imagine anything more exciting...(yawn...)

In spite of his mild demeanor, Jimmy can get angry sometimes. A few decades back, I mentioned that The Beatles were coming to Florida...Jimmy said: 'Damned insects – I'll get the bug spray.' – That's nothing compared to what he does when he REALLY puts some kid in his place! You know the kind I'm talking about: 'What? Who? Man, you better get outta my face. I KNOW you ain't talkin' to ME!!'

That's when Dowirtee goes into his RAP MODE:

> "My name is Jimmy, and I come to say,
> I'm gonna kill everybody this live-long day,
> And, if you don't believe that my story is true,
> Stick around little boy,
> I'M GONNA KILL YOU, TOO!!
> (ra-ra-ra-ra-ra-ra-ra) (ra-ra-ra-ra-ra-ra-ra)

Ya know, folks Kooper & Dowirtee both have mechanical skills, and one summer, when they both failed to get summer school jobs, they worked at a local gas station. One day due to a failure to communicate, they damned near wound up in jail! Seems like this sweet, shall we say voluptuous, young lady drove up in her red-hot convertible. Max & Jimmy, of course, ran to the car, and said: 'HI! Can we help you??!' (VYL): "Hello, Big boys...I want you to check my headlights, I want you to check my taillights, and I want you to check everything in between, bumper-to-bumper!!'...Don't know how they did it, but somehow they managed to convince the judge that they really did not know she meant the ones on the CAR! (Right...ocean-front property in Arizona...)

Next car came in, and again, communication problem: Car's ignition system needed attention. It was a brand new Mercedes, so imagine the driver's surprise when Max and Jimmy opened the hood, stared blankly, and said, 'Yep – the generator won't gen, the carburetor won't carb, the spark plugs won't spark, and the pistons won't...uh...work either!!...Needless to say, the gas station manager let them both go before he went out of business altogether!!!

But, I have to admit, Jimmy did my evaluations a few times, and he was really quite kind to me. Once my psychology class was discussing the human body: how it has evolved; the function of some parts; if you could, how would you alter or improve it, etc. We had some typically cool answers: eye in the back of your head; third arm or hand; gills to breathe underwater. Interesting, I thought, when one kid in the back said, 'Mr "A", I think I would place my ears on the palms of my hands...I said, Gosh, WHY WOULD YOU DO THAT??...He said, so that in January, when it's 26 degrees, I can put them in my pockets and keep them warm...

Well, I was about to award him the trophy, when another kid said, 'Nah...I think the belly button is the most important part of the body. Again, "WHY"? He said, 'Well, I like to eat in bed and that's where I KEEP MY SALT...(go figure...You INNIES agree and understand; You OUTTIES, reverse the process). I thought I was dog meat, but Gentle Jimmy let me slide. I thank you for that, friend, -- and Jimmy "The Legend" Dowirtee, Fletcher thanks you and will miss you for real, Pal!!

• •

And who else will Fletcher miss?? Well, good luck, Senators. Good luck in replacing two hundred years of experience. Good luck in finding a new principal – (gosh, it took us six years to break in Loni!). Three English teachers....(okay, Language Arts — Jeez!!) including a department chairman!! A band director! A librarian...sorry Norzell...I just can't say 'Media Specialist'! Two guidance counselors! AND THE SOCIAL STUD of social studies! And they'll take with them a memory bank that'll top ANY computer! Good Luck, Fletcher High School!!

[I have tried to avoid an excess of inside and/or personal jokes or private references. It has been difficult. There are so many juicy stories and tidbits I could have told about all the people in my life. Even mentioning them to myself mentally gave me several moments to pause and chuckle. Should I, or should I not?? And, even though my efforts at camouflage were shallow at times, I truly meant well. These final entries in my book are quite personal and easily recognizable by most anyone's imagination. Think of any season, school, decade, friend, stadium, barracks, neighborhood, age, fad, crazy-good-time-rite-of-passage, 'when I was a kid' happening or situation — and this little sojourn will certainly give you a chance to reminisce.]

Sooo, kick back and take this trip with me down memory lane:

If you were a kid in the 1940's, 50's, or 60's, you spent a lot of time with radio, concerts, movies, sports, and television. Check out these music makers: — Elvis Presley, The Beatles, Rosemary Clooney, Duke Ellington, B.B. King, Ella Fitzgerald, Hank Williams, Johnny Cash, Frankie Laine, Tony Bennett, Bing Crosby, Bill Haley & The Comets, The Four Freshmen, Kingston Trio, Peggy Lee, Dave Brubeck, Perry Como, Connie Francis, Fats Domino, Little Richard, Chuck Berry, Frank Sinatra, Everly Bros., Andrews Sisters, McGuire Sisters, Ramsey Lewis, Harry James, The Platters, Four Tops, Temptations, and Sarah Vaughn.

How about The Jocks?? Yogi, Mantle, Maris, Ali, Dr. J., Johnny Weismuller, Wilma Rudolph, Hank Aaron, Gordie Howe, Althea Gibson, Bart Starr, George Blanda, Al Kaline, Joe DiMaggio, Ted Williams, Sandi Koufax, Don Drysdale, Willie Mays, Jim Brown, Vince Lombardi, Fran Tarkenton, Johnny Unitas, Bob Cousey, Bill Russell, Jack, Gary, and Arnie, Jesse Owens, Babe Ruth, and Babe Zaharias.

Movie Giants: — Cowboys, Heroes, Villains, and, The Beauties: Such as, — Roy Rogers, Gene Autry, Johnny Mack Brown, Hopalong Cassidy, Red Ryder, Durango Kid, — and their sidekicks, Smiley Burnett, George "Gabby" Hayes, "Fuzzy" St. John, Andy Divine, and Little Beaver.

AND, "The Duke"- John Wayne, James Cagney, Humphrey Bogart, Jimmy Stewart, William Holden, Robert Mitchum, Cary Grant, Gregory Peck, Henry Fonda, Gary Cooper, Tyrone Power, Paul Newman, and, of course, Clark 'Frankly, my dear, I don't give a damn' Gable.

The Scary Guys: — Lon Chaney, Bela Lugosi, Peter Lorre, Sydney Greenstreet, Claude Raines, Boris Karloff, Richard Widmark, Jack Palance, Victor Jory, George Raft, Edward G. Robinson, Vincent Price, and The Master — Alfred Hitchcock.

And The Lovelies, — Marilyn Monroe, Lauren Bacall, Susan Hayward, Jane Russell, Ingrid Bergman, Lee Remick, Doris Day, Liz Taylor, Jayne Mansfield, Betty Grable, Kathryn Hepburn, Rita Hayworth, Lana Turner, and of course... Shirley Temple.

The Funny Teams of Bud Abbott & Lou Costello, The Three Stooges, The Bowery Boys (Deadend Kids), Jack Lemmon & Walter Matthau, Dean Martin & Jerry Lewis, and Bob Hope, Bing Crosby, and Dorothy Lamour--- Toss in a dash of the magic of Walt Disney Features, and Warner Brothers' voice of Mel Blanc for flavor.

The Radio and Television Greats: — Howdy-Doody, Dick Clark & the American Bandstand, The Mouseketeers, Ozzie & Harriet, Leave It To Beaver, Batman & Robin, The Lone Ranger & Tonto, Superman, Wonder Woman, Milton Berle, Red Skelton, Mary Tyler Moore and Dick Van Dyke, Lucille Ball, Sid Caesar, Green Hornet and Cato, Inner Sanctum, Squeaking Door, Carol Burnett, Jack Benny, Flip Wilson, Johnny Carson, Jackie Gleason, Kukla, Fran & Ollie.

There was no multiplex back then. All single screen theaters. The closest we came was the old Normandy Drive-In which had two screens, back to back. Ahh yes... The Drive-In Theater... The Passion Pit... Where we all discovered the wondrous joys of anatomy... 'Gosh! They really ARE built differently than we are!'....Heavy breathing....Foggy windows! Today, it's all we can do to try to stop them from laying down a towel on the floor between the lockers, between classes, and... well, you know!... Okay, they don't always use a towel!!!... Okay! They do it in the classroom!!... Don't know whether to reprimand the fifth grader or his teacher!!....Jeez!...

Remember Movie Row, Downtown, Jax? Main Street started it

with the Capitol and Temple Theaters. When it met Forsyth Street, you would find The St. John's, Arcade, Empress, Imperial (House of Return Hits), Palace, and of course, The Florida Theater – still intact and functioning. But most of us went to the neighborhood theater every Saturday. Depending on where you lived, you went to The Brentwood in Springfield (that was me), Fairfax (Kooper), Arlington (Allbirt), Town & Country, San Marco, Edgewood, Murray Hill, Ritz, Strand, Roosevelt, or down here you went to The Beach Theater,--down there by the Old Board Walk.

If you've heard this before, please hang in there with me... it bears repeating. For four safe hours on any given Saturday at noon, you could WALK (can you imagine that?)...WALK to the theater matinee, without fear of rape, kidnapping, drive-by shooting, purse-snatching, murder, robbery, drug dealers, or mugging, and for 25 cents, here's what you would get: nine cents would be the price of the ticket, 10 cents would buy you a BIG BOX of popcorn, five cents would buy a BIG BAR of candy, — (Butterfinger, Baby Ruth, Mars, Clark Bar, Whiz, O-Henry, Nonpareils, Milk Duds, Jujubees, Mounds Bar, Almond Joy, or Heath Bar)... and with your left over penny, a BIG piece of one-cent candy, like Tootsie Roll, licorice stick, fireball — cinnamon-red-hot-jaw-breaker (remember jaw-breakers? WOW!), or chocolate covered coconut. AANNDDDD, you would be able to see a great double feature, (new movies every week), previews of coming attractions, newsreel, cartoon, and chapter 13 of a serial... "Nyoka, The Jungle Girl," or "The Vigilantes", or "The Man From Planet X" each ending in a cliff hanger for 15 chapters...Those WERE the days, my friends.

Loni Monn is getting her new assignment just in time, it seems. Just last week, downtown sent her the following candidates to interview to replace you retirees: Sponge Bob, The Geico Gecko, The Serta Mattress Sheep, a thimble, and a pair of shoe laces. — Next week, she's supposed to talk to The Pillsbury Doughboy, NBC Peacock, a set of twin pencils, The Energizer Bunny, and the Aflac Duck!! So far, the Duck has the inside track, so, you can see, there's not a whole lot out there, folks. Gosh, if the School Board would only send her someone, ANYONE, who could read, write, talk, and count...(kind of helps explain why she has promised free beer in the water coolers).

YES, my friends, you ARE leaving a big hole in The Fletcher High School Faculty!! YES! You have been tagged as "just being teachers". YES, them that can DO, and them that can't — TEACH!!... Wouldn't you just love to see those condescending jerks try teaching for two years?? They wouldn't last two weeks, two days, or two hours!

My brother Louie fancied himself an amateur philosopher and always used to say, "I can excuse anything except stupidity!" In Arabic, one of his favorite expressions was 'La ijhoosh fe thayta, bit ghut-il-ayn-il-shums'!! Loose translation – 'If jackasses could fly, we would never see the sun'!!

And even in retirement, your educator's mind will still be asking the ancient questions; the forever unanswerable (and not totally original) ten:

1. Just what is Victoria's Secret?... Her TV commercials do not leave a whole lot to the imagination as it is!!

2. Finding yourself in the middle of a staircase... were you going up, or going down? and why were you going?

3. If women get their hair done every few months, why do they call it a permanent?

4. Why is a foundational garment for an eleven-year old girl called a training bra? What are they training?... And, TRAINING TO DO WHAT??

5. Why do we park on a driveway, and drive on a parkway?

6. How do they grow seedless fruit?

7. Why is a fully completed standing structure called a BUILDING?

8. Why are plastic containers for water called GLASSES?

9. Why do mirrors always reflect left to right, but NEVER top to bottom?

10. And finally, why is it when a teacher has an itch in the middle of his brain, the only way he can scratch it is to think about sandpaper??? (Thank you, Steven Wright!)

INQUIRING MINDS WANT TO KNOW!!

I started teaching in 1963-64. My first year's salary was $4,350... NOT a misprint.

My second year's salary (1964-65) — $4355...NOT a misprint. I NEARLY sent the five bucks back to them thinking they probably needed it more than I did. It took me 25 years (20 of those with a Master's Degree!!) to have an annual salary of $25,000. So, now they're wondering why there seems to be a teacher shortage looming on the horizon...But, have faith, my friends. Our Illustrious School Board has come up with a list of ten ways to counteract the expected shortage:

1. Require more paper work in triplicate...'Yes, I need fourteen of those YESTERDAY...OR, in ten minutes — WHICHEVER COMES THIRD!'

2. Have more benchmarks, rubrics, standards, and curriculum on display, just in case you can still determine what color the walls and your desk are, (or were); forget the fact that you just gave EVERY student a detailed syllabus of the course.

3. Be sure you try AT LEAST THREE INTERVENTIONS, before you refer a kid for discipline; just place a record of it in his extended portfolio: 'Now, Freddy — put down that chain saw and let's talk.'

4. 'No pencil? Not to worry. Yes, I DO have another pencil for you'. Of course, that makes 11 pencils you've given Freddy this week. You know brother Steev Ortee, always follows the rules. Said he gave out 7,488 pencils in three weeks!

5. This is Nan & Barbie's favorite: A kid enters Fletcher High School having been in 13 schools in the last three months. BUT, he does know that Florida is a peninsular southern state, 2X=10, snow and rain are forms of precipitation, and that English, NOT Spanish OR Ebonics, is the official language of the United States. And , there you have it, folks — "VOILA"!! He gets a "C" in Social Studies, Math, Science, & Language Arts!! [Right — blame those folks downtown who work in the 'Ivory Tower']. The system calls for the forced entry of some regardless of circumstances.

6. Maintain (& increase) the number of Alphabet Soup Programs: BPO, PPO, CPO, FLT, MLST, LAP, F-CAT, SIP, SDM, ACT, ABC & the XYZ!! Gosh!! FDR would have been delighted!!

7. Expecting you to spend countless hours as extra-curricular sponsors, and never considering the countless hours of overtime you spend week in and week out ALL without recompense. I wonder if Coca Cola or General Motors operate like that??

8. Make sure every kid fully realizes that there is no such thing as failure... only success, progress, and advancement in another direction. Miracle Workers Of The World, Unite! You have nothing to lose but your sanity!

9. Continue to expect you to be as efficient as Bill Gates, Ted Turner, and Donald Trump while continuing to pay teachers that paltry, pittance they call your salary!! And, although none of you went into teaching for the money, you DID expect to earn a living at least!! You know -- put bread on the table!!

10. Jon Phryerr, Ah yes — 'America's Choice' — estimates 116 teachers will retire this year. Now, folks, I'm no Pythagoras, but, if I'm not mistaken, Duval county has approximately 170 schools in the system. If the average is ONE... and Fletcher has EIGHT,... C'mon, Jon-Boy, — DO THE MATH. Sooo, number ten would be to maintain a non-decisive Superintendent whose comb-over will soon include his eyebrows, moustache, and beard!!

• •

Many good folks have come and gone through the Fletcher Connection. Who knows?

Maybe we will meet them some day in that great faculty meeting in the sky. Yes, I have sometimes been called Billy-The-IC-Man, because the words they use to describe me all end in IC... Caustic, Sarcastic, Sardonic, Skeptic, and above all, CYNIC!! Add to the m(ic)x — Arthritic, Chocoholic, Diabetic, Melancholic, and Athletic (?.... I can spell ESPN) — I plead guilty to them all. I love you dearly and do enjoy picking on you, and let me tell you something folks... Sometimes, it's all you can hope for (as my buddy Chollee used to say), to teach these kids to 'Wash your hands, and don't kill people!!' And, if you've done that, you've done one Hell of a good job... TAKE MY WORD!! And, don't let ANYBODY tell you different! Take good care, Fletcher. I appreciate your asking me to come to be the MC, and especially for putting up with me. To my friends, the retirees, to Loni, and to all of you Larger-Than-Life Purple People, I wish you GODSPEED. Thanks again, and Bon Voyage!!

● ●

...Now, I'm not saying that loafing is an absolute art – Oh Hell!! Yes, I am!! Loafing is an absolute art! — One I have mastered over the past few years. Teachers have earned the right to relax – whatever that means to each of them. Teachers never get an Awards Show. (Well — OKAY, they do have an 'Of The Year' Award); very few trophies; and rarely does proper recognition and/or monetary payment come their way.

Yet, as maligned as they often are, they're the ones who are always there to teach children to read, write, count, and THINK; to grow up to be social and productive beings; and hopefully, better than average citizens of the world. To them, I tip my hat.

TAKE A BOW, TEACH!

Epilogue

Gentle Reader,

You have heard it more than once: Animals are smarter than people. Fact is, that man IS an animal – one who is SUPPOSED to be at the top of the Tree of Life. He thinks. He says. He does. Not so peculiar that he, too, is often part of the (observed/observing) population which inhabits the planet, alias, The Earth, alias, The Back Yard Zoo.

The Back Yard Zoo can be found in anybody's back yard, zoo, stadium, church, local grocery store, school, public park, concert hall, neighborhood, or shopping mall. People watching is a very popular pastime. The human specie is a peculiar breed to say the least. People are funny, fun to watch, and even more fun to talk about.

You have probably not found a pattern of 'stream of consciousness' by the likes of William Faulkner or Phillip Roth in my book. I have written nothing so profound as that. However, if, at times, it seems that I covered some topics with tongue-in-cheek, in the vein of America's great humorists (Mark Twain, Will Rogers, Andy Rooney, Garrison Keillor) – that effort was absolutely deliberate. And, I feel that my 'stream of enjoyable snippets' has helped me to fulfill a life-long dream of being published. You have my deepest gratitude for helping make that dream a reality.

If laughter is the best medicine, then perhaps I have written at least one prescription that works. If I made you smile, frown, laugh, angry, happy, sad, reminisce, or merely gave you food for thought – well, then, maybe I've done something right, and that truly is delightful.

Thank you for reading my book. I really appreciate it, and hope you enjoyed it.

Sincerely,

Bill Abdelnour

Bill Abdelnour

William Abdelnour
Bio Sketch

Born in Detroit, Michigan, 1937 son of two Syrian immigrants,
Tony and Della Abdelnour
Lived in Jacksonville, Florida since 1947

Education:

A.A.	Transition from Jacksonville Junior College to Jacksonville University	1957
B.A.	(History) Florida State University	1962
M.A.T.	(Social Studies) Jacksonville University	1967

Military:

USN(R)	1959-1965

Career:

Thirty-nine years teaching in Duval County Florida School System

6th grade	Corinne Scott Elementary School	1963-1966
7th-9th grades	Social Studies - Kirby-Smith Junior High School	1966-1969
9th-12th grades	Social Studies - Duncan U. Fletcher Senior High School	1969-2002

U.S. History and High School Review
Intermittently After School and Evenings (1970's & 1980's)
(Florida Community College at Jacksonville)
U.S. Naval Base – (Mayport, Florida)
Also Certified Administration/Supervision (K – 12)

Family:

Married to the marvelous Helen Eyer Abdelnour since 1971. We have two marvelous daughters: Jennifer Abdelnour and Emily Abdelnour (Allen). We have two marvelous grandchildren, Audrey and Brady Allen and an equally marvelous son-in-law, Eric Allen.